Freshwater Fish of Georgia

FIELD GUIDE

by Dave Bosanko

Adventure Publications
Cambridge, Minnesota

ACKNOWLEDGEMENTS

Special thanks to the Dave Bierman from the Iowa Department of Natural Resources for reviewing this book. Thanks are also due to the United States Fish and Wildlife Service and the Georgia Department of Natural Resources.

Edited by Brett Ortler

Cover and book design by Jonathan Norberg

Illustration credits by artist and page number:
Cover illustrations: Redear Sunfish (main) and Largemouth Bass (upper front cover and back cover) by Duane Raver/USFWS

Timothy Knepp/USFWS: 106 (main), 108 **Julie Martinez:** 42, 48, 60, 64, 70 (bottom), 90, 92, 126 **MyFWC.com/fishing:** 11 **Duane Raver/USFWS:** 10 (both), 19, 22, 24, 26, 28, 30, 32, 34, 36, 38, 44, 46, 50, 52, 56. 72, 86, 100, 114, 116, 118, 120, 130 (both), 132, 142, 144, 150, 154, 156, 158, 160, 162, 164, 166, 168, 174, 176, 178, 180, 182 **Joseph Tomelleri:** 40 (both), 54, 58, 62, 66 (both), 68, 70 (top), 74 (both), 78, 80 (both), 82, 84, 86, 88 (both), 94, 96, 98, 102, 104 (both), 106 (inset), 110, 112, 118, 122, 124, 128, 134, 136, 138, 140, 146, 148, 152, 170, 172

10 9 8 7 6 5 4 3 2

Freshwater Fish of Georgia Field Guide
Copyright © 2010 by Dave Bosanko
Published by Adventure Publications
An imprint of AdventureKEEN
310 Garfield Street South
Cambridge, Minnesota 55008
(800) 678-7006
www.adventurepublications.net
Printed in China
ISBN 978-1-59193-263-5 (pbk.)

TABLE OF CONTENTS

HOW TO USE THIS BOOK

Your *Fish of Georgia Field Guide* is designed to make it easy to identify more than 87 species of the most common and important fish in Georgia and learn fascinating facts about each species' range, natural history and more.

The fish are organized by family, such as Catfish (*Ictaluridae*), Perch (*Percidae*) and Sunfish (*Centrarchidae*). Each family is then listed in alphabetical order. Within these families, individual species are arranged alphabetically in their appropriate groups. For example, members of the Sunfish family are divided into the Black Bass, Crappie and True Sunfish groups. For a detailed list of fish families and individual species, turn to the Table of Contents (pg. 3); the Index (pg. 187) provides a reference guide to fish by common name (such as Lake Trout) and other common terms for the species.

Fish Identification

Determining a fish's body shape is the first step to identifying it. Each fish family usually exhibits one or sometimes two basic outlines. Catfish have long, stout bodies with flattened heads, barbels or "whiskers" around the mouth, a relatively tall but narrow dorsal fin and an adipose fin. There are two forms of Sunfish: the flat, round, plate-like outline we see in Bluegills and the torpedo or "fusiform" shape of Largemouth Bass.

In this field guide you can quickly identify a fish by first matching its general body shape to one of the fish family silhouettes listed in the Table of Contents (pp. 3–7). From there, turn to that family's section and use the illustrations and text descriptions to identify your fish. Sample Pages (pp. 22–23) are provided to explain how the information is presented in each two-page spread.

For some species, the illustration will be enough to identify your catch, but it is important to note that your fish may not look exactly like the artwork. Fish frequently change colors. Males that are brightly colored during the spawning season may show muted coloration at other times. Likewise, bass caught in muddy streams show much less pattern than those taken from clear lakes—and all fish lose some of their markings and color when removed from the water.

Most fish are similar in appearance to one or more other species—often, but not always, within the same family. For example, the Redeye Bass is remarkably similar to the Shoal Bass. To accurately identify such look-alikes, check the inset illustrations and accompanying notes below the main illustration, under the "Similar Species" heading.

Throughout *Fish of Georgia* we use basic biological and fisheries management terms that refer to physical characteristics or conditions of fish and their environment, such as dorsal fin or turbid water. For your convenience, these are listed and defined in the Glossary (pg. 184) along with other handy fish-related terms and their definitions.

Understanding such terminology will help you make sense of reports on state and federal research, fish population surveys, lake assessments, management plans and other important fisheries documents.

FISH ANATOMY

It's much easier to identify fish if you know the names of the different parts of a fish. For example, it's easier to use the term "adipose fin" to indicate the small, soft, fleshy flap on a Catfish's back than to try to describe it. The following illustrations point out the basic parts of a fish; the accompanying text defines these characteristics.

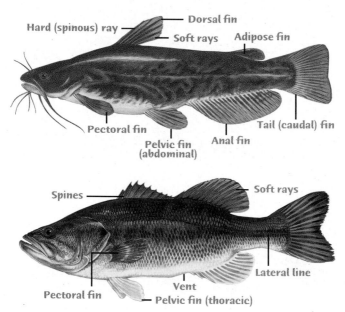

Fins are made up of bony structures that support a membrane. There are three kinds of bony structures in fins:
Soft rays are flexible fin supports and are often branched.

Spines are stiff, often sharp, supports that are not jointed. **Hard rays** are stiff, pointed, barbed structures that can be raised or lowered. Catfish are famous for their hard rays, which are often mistakenly called spines. Sunfish have soft rays associated with spines to form a prominent dorsal fin.

Fins are named by their position on the fish. The **dorsal fin** is on top along the midline. A few species have another fin on their back, called an **adipose fin**. This small, fleshy protuberance located between the dorsal fin and the tail is distinctive of catfish, trout and salmon. **Pectoral fins** are found on each side of the fish near the gills. The **anal fin** is located along the midline, on the fish's bottom or *ventral* side. There is also a paired set of fins on the bottom of the fish, called the **pelvic fins**. These can be in the **thoracic position** (just below the pectoral fins) or farther back on the stomach, in the **abdominal position**. The tail is known as the **caudal fin**.

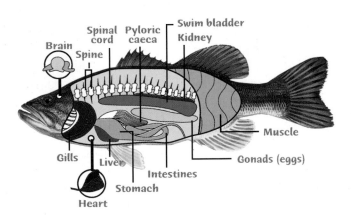

Eyes—In general, fish have good eyesight. They can see color, but the light level they require to see well varies by species. For example, Walleyes see well in low light, whereas Bluegills have excellent daytime vision but see poorly at night, making them vulnerable to predation.

Nostrils—A pair of nostrils, or nares, is used to detect odors in the water. Eels and Catfish have particularly well-developed senses of smell.

Mouth—The shape of the mouth is a clue to what the fish eats. The larger the food it consumes, the larger the mouth.

Teeth—Not all fish have teeth, but those that do have mouthgear designed to help them feed. Gars, Pickerels and Bowfins have sharp canine teeth for grabbing and holding prey. Minnows have *pharyngeal* teeth—located in the throat—for grinding. Catfish have *cardiform* teeth, which feel like a rough patch in the front of the mouth. Bass have patches of *vomerine* teeth on the roof of their mouth.

Swim Bladder—Almost all fish have a swim bladder, a balloon-like organ that helps the fish regulate its buoyancy.

Lateral Line—This sensory organ helps the fish detect movement in the water (to help avoid predators or capture prey) as well as water currents and pressure changes. It consists of fluid-filled sacs with hair-like sensors, which are open to the water through a row of pores in their skin along each side—creating a visible line along the fish's side.

FISH NAMES

A Shellcracker is a Shellcracker in the south, but in the northern parts of its range it is called a Redear Sunfish. In other regions it's known as a stumpknocker or a yellow bream. Because common names may vary regionally, and even change for different sizes of the same species, scientific names are used that are exactly the same around the world. Each species has only one correct scientific name that can be recognized anywhere, in any language. The Largemouth Bass is *Micropterus salmoides* from Atlanta to Athens. Scientific names are made up of Greek or Latin words that often describe the species. There are two parts to a scientific name: the generic or "genus," which is capitalized (*Micropterus*), and the specific name, which is not capitalized (*salmoides*). Both are always written in italic text or underlined. A species' genus represents a group of closely related fish. The Largemouth and Smallmouth Bass are in the same genus, so they share the generic name *Micropterus*. But each fish has a different specific name, *salmoides* for Largemouth Bass, *dolomieu* for the Smallmouth Bass.

ABOUT FISH OF GEORGIA

Georgia is a state blessed with a wide variety of freshwater habitat. In the southeast, there are large coastal rivers, as well as small brackish marshes and ponds. In the north, there are cold mountain streams and clear, deep lakes. In between, there are hundreds of lakes and the famous Okefenokee Swamp. Some of Georgia's lakes are natural oxbows, whereas others are man-made, including small, private ponds and some extensive reservoirs. All of this water provides a range of habitats for fish; this multitude of habitats, when coupled with Georgia's geographic position in the mid-latitudes, means an unusually large number of fish species are found in Georgia.

There are over 200 species of freshwater fish in Georgia, and a few marine fish enter fresh water seasonally to spawn or feed. 87 species are included in this book. About 30 of these species are commonly targeted by anglers, and another 40 or so are of interest to anyone that spends time near the water. Some of these fish are secretive and seldom seen; others are commonly encountered, if only in the bait pail. All of them feature interesting characteristics, and learning about them will help you enjoy your time around the water more fully.

FREQUENTLY ASKED QUESTIONS

What is a fish?

Fish are aquatic, typically cold-blooded animals that have backbones, gills and fins.

Are all fish cold-blooded?

All freshwater fish are cold-blooded. Recently, it has been discovered that some members of the saltwater Tuna family are warm-blooded. Whales and Bottlenose Dolphins are also warm-blooded, but they are mammals, not fish.

Do all fish have scales?

No. Most fish have scales that look like those on the Common Goldfish. A few, such as the Alligator Gar, have scales that resemble armor plates. Catfish have no scales at all.

How do fish breathe?

A fish takes in water through its mouth and forces it through its gills, where a system of fine membranes absorbs oxygen from the water and releases carbon dioxide. Gills cannot pump air efficiently over these membranes, which quickly dry out and stick together. Fish should never be out of the water longer than you can hold your breath.

Can fish breathe air?

Some species can; gars have a modified swim bladder that acts like a lung. Fish that can't breathe air may die when dissolved oxygen in the water falls below critical levels.

How do fish swim?

Fish swim by contracting bands of muscles on alternate sides of their body so the tail is whipped rapidly from side to side. Pectoral and pelvic fins are used mainly for stability when a fish hovers, but are sometimes used during rapid bursts of forward motion.

Do all fish look like fish?

Most do and are easily recognizable as fish. The eels and lampreys are fish, but they look like snakes. Sculpins look like little goblins with bat wings.

Where can you find fish?

Some fish species can be found in almost any body of water, but not all fish are found everywhere. Each species has adapted to exploit a particular habitat. A species may move around within its home water, sometimes migrating hundreds of miles between lakes, rivers and tributary streams. Some movements, such as spawning migrations, are seasonal and very predictable.

Fish may also move horizontally from one area to another, or vertically in the water column in response to changes in environmental conditions and food availability. In addition, many fish have daily travel patterns. By studying a species' habitat, food and spawning information in this book—and understanding how it interacts with other fish—it is possible to guess where one can find it in any lake, stream or river.

FISH DISEASES

Fish are susceptible to various parasites, infections and diseases. Some diseases have little effect on fish populations while others may have a devastating impact. While fish diseases can't be transmitted to humans, they may render the fish inedible. To prevent the spread of such diseases, care should be taken in not transferring diseased fish from one body of water to another. Information on freshwater fish diseases in Georgia can be found at the Georgia Department of Natural Resources' website: www.gadnr.org.

INVASIVE SPECIES

While some introduced species have great recreational value, many exotic species have caused problems. Never move fish, water or vegetation from one lake or stream to another, and always follow state laws. Details about invasive species are available at the Georgia Department of Natural Resources' website: www.gadnr.org.

FUN WITH FISH

There are many ways to enjoy the Fish of Georgia, from reading about them in this book to watching them in the wild. Hands-on activities are also popular. Many resident and nonresident anglers enjoy pursuing game fish. The sport offers a great chance to enjoy the outdoors with friends and family, and in many cases, bring home a healthy meal of fresh fish.

Proceeds from license sales, along with special taxes anglers pay on fishing supplies and motorboat fuel, fund the majority of fish management efforts, including fish surveys, the development of special regulations and stocking programs. The sport also has a huge impact on the economy of Georgia, supporting thousands of jobs in fishing, tourism and related industries.

CATCH-AND-RELEASE FISHING

Selective harvest (keeping some fish to eat and releasing the rest) and total catch-and-release fishing allow anglers to enjoy the sport without harming the resource. Catch-and-release is especially important with certain species and sizes of fish in waters where biologists are trying to improve the fishery by protecting large predators, adult fish, or fish of breeding age. The fishing regulations and information available at your local fisheries offices are excellent sources of advice on which fish to keep and which to release.

Catch-and-release is only truly successful if the fish survives. Follow these helpful tips to reduce the chances of post-release mortality.

- Play and land fish quickly.

- Wet your hands before touching a fish, to avoid removing its protective slime coating.

- Handle the fish gently and keep it in the water if possible.

- Do not hold the fish by the eye sockets or gills. Hold it horizontally and support its belly.

- If a fish is deeply hooked, cut the line so at least an inch hangs outside the mouth. This helps the hook lie flush when the fish takes in food.

- Circle hooks may help reduce deeply hooked fish.

- Don't fish deep in water unless you plan to keep your catch.

FISH MEASUREMENT

Fish are measured in three ways: standard length, fork length and total length. The first two are more accurate, because tails are often damaged or worn down. Total length is used in slot limits.

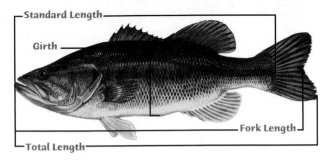

The following formulas estimate the weight of popular game fish. Lengths are in inches; weight is in pounds.

Formulas

Bass weight = (length x length x girth) / 1,200
Pike weight = (length x length x length) / 3,500
Sunfish weight = (length x length x length) / 1,200
Trout weight = (length x girth x girth) / 800
Walleye weight = (length x length x length) / 2,700

For example, let's say that you catch a 16-inch Walleye. Using the formula for Walleyes above: (16 x 16 x 16) divided by 2,700 = 1.5 pounds. Your Walleye would weigh approximately 1.5 pounds.

FISH CONSUMPTION ADVISORIES

Most fish are safe to eat, but pollutants are a valid concern. Georgia routinely monitors contaminant levels and issues advisories and recommendations about eating sport fish caught in the wild. For information contact Georgia Department of Natural Resources' Environmental Protection Division at (404) 656-4713, or www.gaepd.org

GEORGIA STATE RECORD FISH

SPECIES	WEIGHT (LBS.-OZ.)	WHERE CAUGHT	YEAR
Bass, Largemouth	22-4	Montgomery Lake	1932
Bass, Redeye	3-7	Lake Hartwell	2004
Bass, Shoal	8-3	Flint River	1977
Bass, Smallmouth	7-2	Lake Chatuge	1973
Bass, Spotted	8-2	Lake Burton	2005
Bass, Striped	63-0	Oconee River	1967
Bass, Striped Hybrid	25-8	Lake Chatuge	1995
Bass, Suwannee	3-9	Ochlocknee River	1984
Bass, White	5-1	Lake Lanier	1971
Bowfin	16-0	Stephen Foster State Park	1976
Bullhead, Brown	5-8	O.F. Veal Pond	1978
Bullhead, Yellow	4-15	Ogeechee River	2003
Catfish, Blue	67-8	Chattahoochee River	2006
Catfish, Channel	44-12	Altamaha River	1972
Catfish, Flathead	83-0	Altamaha River	2006
Catfish, White	8-10	Savannah River	1996
Carp, Common	35-12	Lake Jackson	1972
Crappie, Black	4-4	Acrees Lake	1971
Crappie, White	5-0	Bibb County Pond	1984
Gar, Longnose	28-6	Flint River	1995
Muskellunge	38-0	Lake Blue Ridge	1957
Pickerel, Chain	9-6	Homerville	1961
Pickerel, Redfin	2-10	Lewis Pond	1982
Pike, Northern	18-2	Lake Rabun	1982
Sauger	4-3	Clarks Hill Lake	1986

SPECIES	WEIGHT (LBS.-OZ.)	WHERE CAUGHT	YEAR
Walleye	11-6	Richard B. Russell Lake	1995
Perch, Yellow	2-8	Lake Burton	1980
Shad, American	8-3	Savannah River	1986
Shad, Hickory	1-15	Ogeechee River	1995
Bluegill	3-5	Shamrock Lake	1977
Flier	1-4	Lowndes County Pond	1996
Sunfish, Green	1-7	private pond	2006
Sunfish, Redbreast	1-11	Coweta County Pond	1998
Sunfish, Redear	4-2	Richmond County Pond	1995
Sunfish, Spotted	0-10	Brier Creek	2003
Warmouth	2-0	private pond	1974
Trout, Brook	5-10	Waters Creek	1986
Trout, Brown	18-6	Chattahoochee River	2001
Trout, Rainbow	17-8	Soque River	1995

These pages explain how the information is presented for each fish.

SAMPLE FISH ILLUSTRATION

Description: brief summary of physical characteristics to help you identify the fish, such as coloration and markings, body shape, fin size and placement

Similar Species: list of other fish that look similar and the pages on which they can be found; includes detailed inset drawings (below) highlighting key physical traits such as markings, mouth size or shape and fin characteristics to help you distinguish this fish from similar species

Brook Trout	Brown Trout	Rainbow Trout	Lake Trout
worm-like marks, red spots	large dark spots, small red dots	pink stripe on silver body	sides lack red spots

SAMPLE COMPARISON ILLUSTRATIONS

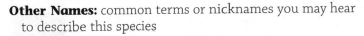

COMMON NAME

Scientific Name

Other Names: common terms or nicknames you may hear to describe this species

Habitat: environment where the fish is found (such as streams, rivers, small or large lakes, fast-flowing or still water, in or around vegetation, near shore, in clear water)

Range: geographic distribution, starting with the fish's overall range, followed by state-specific information

Food: what the fish eats most of the time (such as crustaceans, insects, fish, plankton)

Reproduction: timing of the spawning period and a fish's behavior during it, including spawning dates and water temperatures, migration information, preferred spawning habitat, type of nest (if applicable), whether a fish is a colonial or solitary nester, and whether there is parental care for eggs or fry

Average Size: average length or range of length, average weight or range of weight

Records: state—the state record for this species, location and year; North American—the North American record for this species, location and year; from the National Fresh Water Fishing Hall of Fame, unless noted as IGFA (International Game Fish Association)

Notes: interesting natural history information; this can include unique behaviors, remarkable features, sporting and table quality, details on annual migrations, seasonal patterns or population trends

23

Description: brownish-green back and sides with a white belly; long, stout body; rounded tail; continuous dorsal fin; bony plates covering head; males have a large "eye" spot at the base of the tail

Similar Species: Northern Snakehead (pg. 126)

Bowfin	Northern Snakehead
no head scales, bony plates between jaws	enlarged scales on head

Bowfin	Northern Snakehead
pelvic fins at mid-body, short anal fin	pelvic fins near head, long anal fin

BOWFIN

Amia calva

Other Names: dogfish, grindle, mudfish, cypress trout, lake lawyer, beaverfish, scaly cat

Habitat: deep waters associated with weedbeds in warmwater lakes and rivers; feeds in shallow weeds

Range: the Mississippi River drainage east and south from Texas to Florida; Georgia—coastal lowlands

Food: fish, crayfish

Reproduction: when water exceeds 61 degrees, male removes vegetation to build a nest in sand or gravel; one or more females deposit up to 5,000 eggs; male tenaciously guards the nest and "ball" of young

Average Size: 12 to 24 inches, 2 to 5 pounds

Records: state—16 pounds, Stephen Foster State Park, 1976; North American—21 pounds, 8 ounces, Forest Lake, South Carolina, 1980

Notes: Bowfins are a common native fish of Georgia's coastal lowlands and have been introduced to a few impoundments further north. A voracious predator, the Bowfin prowls shallow weedbeds preying on anything that moves. Once thought detrimental to game fish populations, it is now considered an asset in controlling rough fish and stunted game fish. An air breather that tolerates low oxygen levels, the Bowfin can survive buried in mud for short periods during droughts. While most anglers consider the Bowfin a nuisance, some anglers seek it out for its fighting ability. The flesh has an unusual texture and flavor.

Description: black to olive-green back; sides yellowish-green; belly creamy white to yellow; light bar at base of tail; barbels around mouth dark at base; adipose fin; lacks scales; round tail

Similar Species: Brown Bullhead (pg. 28), Yellow Bullhead (pg. 30), White Catfish (pg. 38), Flathead Catfish (pg. 36), Madtoms (pg. 40)

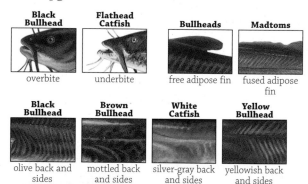

Black Bullhead	**Flathead Catfish**	**Bullheads**	**Madtoms**
overbite	underbite	free adipose fin	fused adipose fin

Black Bullhead	**Brown Bullhead**	**White Catfish**	**Yellow Bullhead**
olive back and sides	mottled back and sides	silver-gray back and sides	yellowish back and sides

BLACK BULLHEAD

Ameiurus melas

Other Names: common bullhead, horned pout

Habitat: shallow, slow-moving streams and backwaters; lakes and ponds—tolerates extremely turbid (cloudy) conditions

Range: southern Canada through the Great Lakes and the Mississippi River watershed to the Southwest and into Mexico; Georgia—northern mountains to central Georgia

Food: a scavenging opportunist; feeds mostly on animal material (dead or alive) but will eat plant matter

Reproduction: spawns from late April to early June; builds nest in shallow water with a muddy bottom; both sexes guard nest, eggs and young to 1 inch in size

Average Size: 8 to 10 inches, 4 ounces to 1 pound

Records: state—none; North American—8 pounds, 15 ounces, Sturgis Pond, Michigan, 1987

Notes: The Black Bullhead is the most widespread and common bullhead species in the central and southern US, and on average, the smallest. It is the rarest bullhead in Georgia. The Black Bullhead is also the bullhead species most tolerant of silt, pollution and low oxygen levels, but its numbers have still decreased since the early twentieth century. As table fare, bullheads get little respect, but they are bigger than most panfish taken home to eat, and are just as tasty.

Description: yellowish-brown upper body; mottled back and sides; barbels around mouth; adipose fin; scaleless body; rounded tail; well-defined barbs on the pectoral spines

Similar Species: Yellow Bullhead (pg. 30), Black Bullhead (pg. 26), Madtoms (pg. 40)

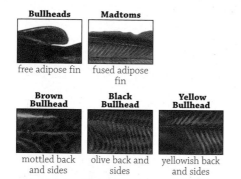

Bullheads	**Madtoms**
free adipose fin	fused adipose fin

Brown Bullhead	**Black Bullhead**	**Yellow Bullhead**
mottled back and sides	olive back and sides	yellowish back and sides

BROWN BULLHEAD

Ameiurus nebulosus

Other Names: marbled or speckled bullhead, red cat

Habitat: warm, weedy lakes and sluggish streams

Range: southern Canada through the Great Lakes and the eastern states to Florida, introduced in the West; Georgia —common statewide

Food: a scavenging opportunist, feeds mostly on insects, fish, fish eggs, snails and some plant matter

Reproduction: in early summer, the male builds a nest in shallow water amid vegetation over a sandy or rocky bottom; both sexes guard the eggs and young

Average Size: 8 to 10 inches, 4 ounces to 2 pounds

Records: state—5 pounds, 8 ounces, private pond, 1978; North American—6 pounds, 2 ounces, Pearl River, Mississippi, 1991

Notes: The Brown Bullhead is a common and abundant catfish in Georgia. They can be found in turbid backwaters as well as in clear lakes and streams. Adults are very involved in rearing their young; first they agitate the eggs, then they guard the black fry, which swim in a tight ball. Like other catfish, Brown Bullheads are primarily nocturnal feeders, but are still often caught during the day. They are not strong fighters, but are easy to catch when fishing the bottom with worms as bait. The reddish meat is tasty and fine table fare when taken from clean water.

Description: dark olive head and back; yellowish-green sides; white belly; barbels on lower jaw are pale green or white; adipose fin; scaleless body; rounded tail

Similar Species: Brown Bullhead (pg. 28), Black Bullhead (pg. 26), Madtoms (pg. 40)

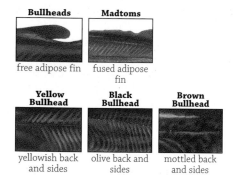

Bullheads	Madtoms
free adipose fin	fused adipose fin

Yellow Bullhead	Black Bullhead	Brown Bullhead
yellowish back and sides	olive back and sides	mottled back and sides

YELLOW BULLHEAD

Ictaluridae

Ameiurus natalis

Other Names: white-whiskered bullhead, yellow cat

Habitat: warm, weedy lakes and sluggish streams

Range: the southern Great Lakes through the eastern half of the US to the Gulf and into Mexico, introduced in the West; Georgia—statewide

Food: scavenging opportunist, feeds on insects, crayfish, snails, small fish, some plant matter

Reproduction: from late spring to early summer, male builds a nest in shallow water amid vegetation with a soft bottom; both sexes guard the eggs and young

Average Size: 8 to 10 inches, 1 to 2 pounds

Records: state—4 pounds, 15 ounces, Ogeechee River, 2003; North American—4 pounds, 15 ounces, Ogeechee River, Georgia, 2003

Notes: The Yellow Bullhead is the bullhead species least tolerant of turbidity and is commonly found in clear streams or ponds. Bullheads feed by "taste," locating food by following chemical trails through the water. This ability can be greatly diminished in polluted water, impairing the bullhead's ability to find food. The Yellow Bullhead is less likely than other bullhead species to overpopulate a lake and become stunted. Yellow Bullheads are easily caught with worms or cut bait throughout the day, but they are more active at night. The creamy, white flesh is firm and tasty when the fish are taken from clean water.

Description: body pale blue to slate gray; hump in back at
dorsal fin; long anal fin with straight rear edge; forked tail;
adipose fin; no scales; chin barbels

Similar Species: Channel Catfish (pg. 34), White Catfish
(pg. 38)

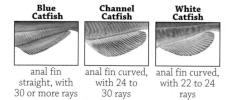

Blue Catfish	Channel Catfish	White Catfish
anal fin straight, with 30 or more rays	anal fin curved, with 24 to 30 rays	anal fin curved, with 22 to 24 rays

BLUE CATFISH
Ictalurus furcatus

Ictaluridae

Other Names: humpback, river, forktail, great blue, silver, chucklehead, or Missouri cat, blue fulton

Habitat: deep pools of large rivers with hard bottoms and moderate to strong current, a few reservoirs

Range: the Mississippi River watershed and into Mexico; Georgia—few large rivers and impoundments

Food: fish, crayfish

Reproduction: spawns when water reaches the low 80s; male builds and defends a nest in undercut banks or other sheltered areas; males guard young for a short period

Average Size: 20 to 30 inches, 15 to 25 pounds

Records: state—67 pounds, 8 ounces, Chattahoochee River, 2006; North American—124 pounds, Mississippi River, Illinois, 2005

Notes: The Blue Catfish is the largest North American catfish. Though not native to Georgia, there is a well-established population in the Chattahoochee River and a few other large tributary streams. Primarily river fish, they prefer fast currents and often congregate in the water below power-generating dams to feed on injured fish that pass through the turbines. Large, old Channel or White Catfish are often mistaken for smaller Blue Cats, as they all have very similar coloration. This has led to a great deal of confusion in some fishing contests. Like other catfish species, Blue Catfish have firm, white flesh that is fine table fare.

33

Description: steel gray to silver on the back and sides; white belly; black spots on the sides; large fish lack spots and appear dark olive or slate gray; forked tail; adipose fin; long barbels around mouth

Similar Species: Bullheads (pp. 26-30), White Catfish (pg. 38), Blue Catfish (pg. 32)

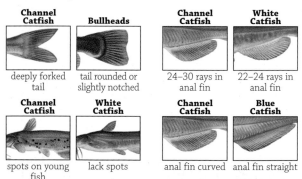

Channel Catfish	Bullheads	Channel Catfish	White Catfish
deeply forked tail	tail rounded or slightly notched	24–30 rays in anal fin	22–24 rays in anal fin

Channel Catfish	White Catfish	Channel Catfish	Blue Catfish
spots on young fish	lack spots	anal fin curved	anal fin straight

CHANNEL CATFISH

Ictalurus punctatus

Other Names: spotted, speckled, or silver catfish, fiddler

Habitat: medium to large streams with deep pools, low to moderate current and sand, gravel or rubble bottom; warm lakes and ponds; tolerates turbid conditions

Range: southern Canada through the Midwest into Mexico and Florida; widely introduced worldwide; Georgia—statewide

Food: insects, crustaceans, fish, some plant matter

Reproduction: matures at 2 to 4 years; in summer when water temperature reaches about 70 to 85 degrees, male builds nest in dark, sheltered areas; female deposits 2,000 to 21,000 eggs, which hatch in 6 to 10 days; male guards eggs and young until the nest is deserted

Average Size: 12 to 20 inches, 3 to 4 pounds

Records: state—44 pounds, 12 ounces, Altamaha River, 1972; North American—58 pounds, Santee Cooper Reservoir, South Carolina, 1964

Notes: Channel Catfish are one of the most sought-after fish in much of the US, and Georgia is no exception. Like other catfish, Channel Catfish feed both day and night, but serious anglers often pursue them at night. When caught, they put up a strong fight and are fine table fare. Channel Catfish were the first widely farmed fish in the US and are now also raised in Asia for export around the world. Channel Catfish are the only native freshwater American fish commonly found in grocery stores and restaurants throughout the country.

Description: color variable, body and head usually mottled yellow or brown; belly cream to yellow; head broad and flattened; pronounced underbite; adipose fin; chin barbels

Similar Species: Blue Catfish (pg. 32), Channel Catfish (pg. 34)

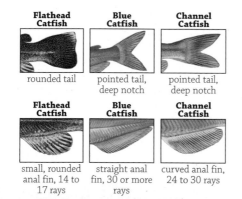

Flathead Catfish	Blue Catfish	Channel Catfish
rounded tail	pointed tail, deep notch	pointed tail, deep notch

Flathead Catfish	Blue Catfish	Channel Catfish
small, rounded anal fin, 14 to 17 rays	straight anal fin, 30 or more rays	curved anal fin, 24 to 30 rays

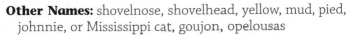

FLATHEAD CATFISH

Pylodictis olivaris

Ictaluridae

Other Names: shovelnose, shovelhead, yellow, mud, pied, johnnie, or Mississippi cat, goujon, opelousas

Habitat: deep pools of large rivers and impoundments

Range: the Mississippi River watershed and the Gulf Slope, south into Mexico; introduced to some Atlantic drainages; Georgia—few large rivers and reservoirs

Food: fish, crayfish

Reproduction: spawns when water is 72 to 80 degrees; male builds and defends nest in hollow logs or undercut banks; large females may lay up to 30,000 eggs

Average Size: 20 to 30 inches, 10 to 20 pounds

Records: state—83 pounds, Altamaha River, 2006; North American—123 pounds, Elk River Reservoir, Kansas, 1998

Notes: Flathead catfish are large solitary predators that feed aggressively on live fish at night. Flatheads are frequently found near logjams or in deep pools where they can hide in cavities during the day. Occasionally Flatheads enter shallow water seeking prey, but they are more likely to stay in deep water and are easily spooked when near the surface. Flatheads have been stocked in small lakes in an attempt to control stunted panfish populations, with limited success. Some of these introductions result in steep declines in popular game fish populations. Flatheads are strong, tenacious fighters with firm, white flesh and are highly prized by many catfish anglers.

37

Description: bluish-silver body and off-white belly; older fish dark blue with some mottling; forked tail with pointed lobes; lacks scales; adipose fin; white chin barbels

Similar Species: Channel Catfish (pg. 34)

White Catfish	**Channel Catfish**	**White Catfish**	**Channel Catfish**
22 to 24 rays in anal fin, no spots	24 to 30 rays in anal fin	always lack spots	spots on young fish

WHITE CATFISH

Ameiurus catus

Other Names: silver or weed catfish, whitey

Habitat: fresh to slightly brackish water of coastal streams; shallow lakes with good vegetation and a firm bottom

Range: Maine south to Florida and west to Texas; introduced in some western states; Georgia—native in eastern drainages, introduced statewide

Food: insects, crayfish, small fish, some plant debris

Reproduction: male builds nest in sheltered areas with a sand or gravel bottom when water temperatures reach the high 60s; both sexes guard nest and eggs until fry disperse

Average Size: 10 to 18 inches, 1 to 2 pounds

Records: state—8 pounds, 10 ounces, Savannah River, 1996; North American—22 pounds, William Land Park Pond, California, 1994

Notes: The White Catfish is a native species that is found in fresh water and slightly brackish coastal waters of Georgia. In terms of habits, White Catfish share characteristics with both Channel Catfish and bullheads. White Catfish prefer quieter water than Channel Catfish and with a somewhat firmer bottom than that sought by bullheads. They are somewhat less nocturnal than other catfish. In terms of popularity with Georgia fishermen, they are second only to the Channel Catfish. They frequent the edge of reed beds and are often caught when still-fishing the bottom near deep water. Large White Catfish put up a good battle and have firm, white flesh with a fine flavor. **39**

TADPOLE MADTOM

MARGINED MADTOM

Description: Margined—gray to tan; protruding upper jaw; squared tail; Tadpole—dark olive to brown; dark line on side; rounded tail; jaws even; fin margins black; both species— large, fleshy head with barbels at mouth; adipose fin connected to tail fin

Similar Species: Bullheads (pp. 26-30), Catfish (pp. 32-38)

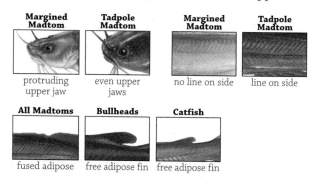

Margined Madtom	Tadpole Madtom	Margined Madtom	Tadpole Madtom
protruding upper jaw	even upper jaws	no line on side	line on side

All Madtoms	Bullheads	Catfish
fused adipose	free adipose fin	free adipose fin

TADPOLE MADTOM
Noturus gyrinus

MARGINED MADTOM *Noturus insignis*

Other Names: Tadpole—willow or tadpole cat, tadpole stonecat; Margined—river or creek madtom

Habitat: Tadpole—vegetated water near shore in medium to large lakes; Margined—rocky stream and creek riffles

Range: Tadpole—the eastern US from the Gulf through the Great Lake states; Georgia—central and eastern lowlands; Margined—Atlantic slope from New York to Georgia; Georgia—northern half of state

Food: small invertebrates, algae and other plant matter

Reproduction: both spawn in late spring; females lay eggs under objects such as roots, rocks, logs, or in abandoned crayfish burrows; nest guarded by adults

Average Size: 3 to 4 inches

Records: none

Notes: There are 9 species of small catfish called madtoms that live in Georgia. The Margined Madtom, like most species in the family, is a stream fish. The Tadpole Madtom is the exception and prefers lakes and ponds. Madtoms have poison glands under their skin at the base of the dorsal and pectoral fins; these produce a painful burning sensation but will do no lasting damage. Madtoms are hardy little fish and a popular baitfish in some areas. Reportedly, damaging the "slime" coating (by rolling them in sand) to make handling easier reduces their effectiveness as bait.

Description: bicolored body, brown above lateral line, creamy white below; 3 dark stripes on sides; flattened head with small eyes; large rounded pectoral fins, no pelvic fins

Similar Species: Eastern Mudminnow (pg. 90)

Swampfish

bicolored, no pelvic fins

Eastern Mudminnow

solid color on sides, pelvic fins

SWAMPFISH

Chologaster cornuta

Amblyopsidae

Other Names: mud or blacktop minnow

Habitat: in vegetation near or on the bottom of swamps, creeks and lakes with darkly stained water

Range: Atlantic coastal plains from Virginia to east-central Georgia; Georgia—coastal lowlands

Food: small crustaceans and aquatic insect larvae

Reproduction: spawns in late spring but little else is known of their breeding behavior

Average Size: 1 to 3 inches

Records: none

Notes: This interesting and attractive member of the cavefish family is adapted to living in the darkly stained waters of swamps and creeks, not caves. Swampfish are secretive, nocturnal bottom dwellers that are never found far from thick vegetation. Adult males develop a small, fleshy appendage on the snout, the function of which is unclear. As with other cavefish species, as the fish matures, the anus of the Swampfish migrates forward from the normal position to just under the gills. This is an adaptation found in fish that brood eggs under the gill covers. Swampfish are not often noticed but they can be very abundant in roadside ditches and swamps.

43

Description: gray back with purple or bronze reflections; silver sides; white underbelly; humped back; dorsal fin extends from hump to near tail; lateral line runs from head through tail

Similar Species: White Bass (pg. 176)

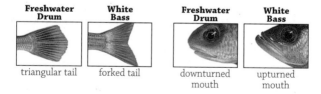

Freshwater Drum	White Bass	Freshwater Drum	White Bass
triangular tail	forked tail	downturned mouth	upturned mouth

FRESHWATER DRUM

Aplodinotus grunniens

Other Names: sheepshead, croaker, thunderpumper, grinder, bubbler; commercially marketed as white perch

Habitat: areas with slow-to-moderate currents in rivers and streams; shallow lakes with soft bottoms; prefers turbid (cloudy) water

Range: Canada south through the Midwest into eastern Mexico to Guatemala; Georgia—northeastern corner

Food: small fish, insects, crayfish, clams, mussels

Reproduction: spawns in May and June after water temperatures reach the mid-60s; schools of drum lay eggs near the surface over sand or gravel; no parental care of eggs or fry

Average Size: 10 to 14 inches, 2 to 5 pounds

Records: state—none; North American—54 pounds, 8 ounces, Nickajack Lake, Tennessee, 1972

Notes: The only freshwater member of a large family of marine fish. Drums are named for a grunting noise that is made by males, primarily to attract females. This noise is occasionally made when a drum is removed from the water and handled. The skull contains two enlarged L-shaped earstones called otoliths that were once prized for jewelry by Native Americans. The flesh is flaky, white and tasty, but easily dries out when cooked due to the low oil content. Flavor of freshwater drum can be improved if the fish is put on ice and chilled as soon as it is caught, and if care is taken to remove all of the reddish-colored flesh from the filets.

Description: dark brown on top with yellow sides and white belly; long, snake-like body with large mouth; pectoral fins; gill slits; continuous dorsal, tail and anal fin

Similar Species: Freshwater Lampreys (pg. 66), Sea Lamprey (pg. 68)

American Eel

continuous dorsal tail, anal fin, no notch in dorsal fin

Sea Lamprey

continuous dorsal tail and anal fin, deeply notched dorsal fin

Freshwater Lampreys

slightly notched dorsal fin

American Eel

pectoral fins

Sea Lamprey

no pectoral fins

AMERICAN EEL

Anguilla rostrata

Other Names: common, Boston, Atlantic or freshwater eel

Habitat: soft bottoms of medium to large streams; brackish tidewater areas

Range: Atlantic Ocean, eastern and central North America and eastern Central America; Georgia—most streams with Atlantic drainage

Food: insects, crayfish, small fish

Reproduction: a "catadromous" species that spends most of its life in fresh water, the American Eel returns to the Sargasso Sea in the North Atlantic Ocean to spawn; females lay up to 20 million eggs; adults die after spawning

Average Size: 24 to 36 inches, 1 to 3 pounds

Records: state—none; North American—8 pounds, 8 ounces, Cliff Pond, Massachusetts, 1992

Notes: Leaf-shaped larval eels drift with ocean currents for about a year after hatching in the Sargasso Sea. When they reach river mouths of North and Central America they morph into small eels (elvers). Males remain in the estuaries; females migrate upstream, often hundreds of miles. At maturity (up to 20 years of age) adults return to the Sargasso Sea. The popularity of eels has decreased in the last 100 years, and now there is only a limited commercial harvest and only a few anglers seek them out. Smoked eels have excellent flavor and are prized in Europe.

Description: olive to brown with dark spots on the head, body and fins; large round spots on top of head; long, cylindrical profile; single dorsal fin located just above the anal fin; body encased in hard, plate-like scales; broad snout; needle-sharp teeth on both jaws

Similar Species: Longnose Gar (pg. 50), Spotted Gar (pg. 52)

Florida Gar	**Longnose Gar**	**Spotted Gar**
distance from front of eye to back of gill less than two-thirds snout length	snout twice the length of the rest of head	distance from front of eye to back of gill more than two-thirds snout length

FLORIDA GAR

Lepisosteidae

Lepisosteus platyrhincus

Other Names: garfish, spotted gar

Habitat: quiet waters of larger rivers and lakes

Range: eastern Florida, north through coastal Georgia to South Carolina; Georgia—southern Georgia north to Savannah River

Food: minnows and other small fish

Reproduction: large, green eggs are deposited in weedy shallows when water temperatures reach the high 60s; using a small disc on the snout, newly hatched gar attach to something solid until their digestive tracts develop enough to allow feeding

Average Size: 18 to 30 inches, 4 to 6 pounds

Records: state—none; North American—9 pounds, 7 ounces, Lake Lawne, Orange County, Florida, 2001

Notes: Very closely related to the Spotted Gar, The Florida Gar is found only in southern Georgia up through the Okefenokee Swamp to the Savannah River. Gar float near the surface waiting to ambush prey with a quick sideways lunge. Florida Gar are never seen very far from brush or other vegetation and frequently congregate in small groups. Gar are good fighters, but hard to hook. The flesh has a very strong, fishy flavor and is not liked by many anglers. Gar eggs are poisonous to mammals but not to other fish.

Description: olive to brown with dark spots along sides;
long, cylindrical profile; single dorsal fin located just above
the anal fin; body encased in hard, plate-like scales; snout
twice as long as head; needle-sharp teeth on both jaws

Similar Species: Florida Gar (pg. 48), Spotted Gar (pg. 52)

Longnose Gar	Florida Gar	Spotted Gar
snout twice the length of the rest of head	distance from front of eye to back of gill less than two-thirds snout length	distance from front of eye to back of gill more than two-thirds snout length

LONGNOSE GAR

Lepisosteus osseus

Other Names: garfish

Habitat: quiet water of larger rivers and lakes

Range: the central US throughout the Mississippi drainage south into Mexico, a few rivers in the northeast Great Lakes drainage; Georgia—possible statewide

Food: minnows and other small fish

Reproduction: large, green eggs are deposited in weedy shallows when water temperature reaches the high 60s; using a small disc on the snout, newly hatched gar attach to something solid until their digestive tracts develop enough to allow feeding

Average Size: 14 to 24 inches, 2 to 4 pounds

Records: state—28 pounds, 6 ounces, Flint River, 1995; North American—50 pounds, 5 ounces, Trinity River, Texas, 1954

Notes: Gar belong to a prehistoric family of fish that can breathe air with the aid of a modified swim bladder. This adaptation helps them survive in increasingly polluted, slow-moving rivers and lakes. Gar are a valuable asset in controlling populations of rough fish. Gar hunt by floating motionless, then make a quick, sideways slash to capture prey. They are tenacious fighters when caught, but their bony jaws make them hard to hook. The flesh is strongly flavored and not popular with most anglers, but gar are frequently targeted by bowfishermen.

Description: Back and sides olive-brown to black-tan below; brown or black spots on head, body and fins; moderately long snout with only one row of teeth on upper jaw; young often have dark stripes on their sides and back

Similar Species: Florida Gar (pg. 48), Longnose Gar (pg. 50)

Spotted Gar	**Florida Gar**	**Longnose Gar**
distance from front of eye to back of gill more than two-thirds snout length	distance from front of eye to back of gill less than two-thirds snout length	snout twice the length of the rest of head

SPOTTED GAR

Lepisosteus oculatus

Other Names: garfish

Habitat: quiet water of larger to medium rivers and lakes with good vegetation

Range: central US throughout the Mississippi drainage to the southern Great Lakes, east to western Florida, west to Texas; Georgia—northeast corner of the state

Food: minnows and other small fish

Reproduction: adhesive eggs are deposited in weedy shallows when water temperatures reach the high 60s; using a small disc on the snout, newly hatched gar attach to something solid until their digestive tracts develop enough to allow feeding

Average Size: 18 to 30 inches, 4 to 6 pounds

Records: state—none; North American—28 pounds, 8 ounces, Lake Seminole, Florida, 1887

Notes: The Spotted Gar is a small gar common to the central US, but it is rare in Georgia. All gar species spend some time in brackish waters and occasionally venture into salt water. Spotted Gar seem to prefer denser vegetation than other gar and often lose their spots in dark-colored water. Small Spotted Gar are popular aquarium fish but need live food to do well.

Description: deep, laterally compressed silver body with blue back; one dark spot on the shoulder just behind the gill; the sharply pointed scales (scutes) along the belly have a sawtooth edge; black lining in body cavity

Similar Species: American Shad (pg. 56), Gizzard Shad (pg. 58)

Blueback Herring	American Shad	Gizzard Shad
black body cavity lining; mouth extends to middle of eye	mouth extends to back of eye	mouth below snout

BLUEBACK HERRING

Alosa aestivalis

Other Names: glut herring

Habitat: coastal marine most of the year; migrates up rivers and streams to spawn; established in some large reservoirs

Range: the Atlantic coast from Nova Scotia to the St. Johns River, Florida, and associated spawning rivers; Georgia— coastal rivers, introduced to inland reservoirs

Food: marine plankton feeder

Reproduction: Blueback Herring are "anadromous" and live in salt water but spawn in fresh water; they migrate to brackish river mouths or upstream to spawn when the water temperature is near 57 degrees; they have an extended spawning season that lasts up to 3 months; eggs are deposited in moving water over sand or gravel

Average Size: 10 to 12 inches, 12 ounces

Records: none

Notes: The Blueback Herring is a marine fish that migrates to fresh water to spawn. Bluebacks may migrate far upstream or spawn in brackish water. Due to their great numbers at stream mouths during spawning season, the Blueback Herring have acquired the name "glut herring." Bluebacks have been stocked in several reservoirs to provide forage for game fish; in others they have become established from released baitfish. Many marine populations of Blueback Herrings seem to be declining, but freshwater populations are expanding.

Description: silver body and blue-gray back; three or more dark spots on the shoulder; body deep and laterally compressed; large mouth extending to back of eye; sawtooth edge of sharply pointed scales along the belly (scutes)

Similar Species: Blueback Herring (pg. 54), Hickory Shad (pg. 60)

American Shad

mouth extends to back of eye; jaws even

Blueback Herring

mouth extends to middle of eye

Hickory Shad

mouth below snout

AMERICAN SHAD

Alosa sapidissima

Other Names: river, silver or white shad

Habitat: coastal marine most of the year; migrates up large rivers to spawn; landlocked in a few areas

Range: the Atlantic coast and spawning rivers from Newfoundland to Florida; Georgia—coastal, ascending large rivers to spawn

Food: plankton, crustaceans, small fish

Reproduction: American Shad migrate upstream when water temperature reaches 62 to 67 degrees; spawning takes place in large rivers at the mouth of tributary streams; in the north, adults return to the sea after spawning; in the south, they often die after spawning

Average Size: 18 to 20 inches, 2 to 3 pounds

Records: state—8 pounds, 3 ounces, Savannah River, 1986; North American—11 pounds, 4 ounces, Connecticut River, Massachusetts, 1986

Notes: The American Shad is a large shad similar to the Hickory Shad. Both species spawn in the same Georgia waters at about the same time. Like other shad, the American Shad makes a spring spawning run; in fact, the American Shad helped save George Washington's starving troops at Valley Forge. Today, the spring run is still an important commercial and sport-fishing event in coastal states. American Shad readily take small artificial lures and have become very popular with fly fishermen. Shad are oily fish that are very good when smoked, baked or fried.

57

Description: deep, laterally compressed body; silvery-blue back with white sides and belly; young fish have a dark spot on shoulder behind the gill; small mouth; last rays of dorsal fin form a long thread

Similar Species: American Shad (pg. 56), Blueback Herring (pg. 54)

Gizzard Shad	American Shad	Blueback Herring
mouth below snout	jaws even	underbite

GIZZARD SHAD

Dorosoma cepedianum

Other Names: hickory, mud or jack shad

Habitat: large rivers, reservoirs, lakes, swamps and temporarily flooded pools; brackish and saline waters in coastal areas

Range: the St. Lawrence, Great Lakes, Mississippi, Atlantic and Gulf Slope drainages from Quebec to Mexico, south to central Florida; Georgia—coastal rivers and large impoundments statewide

Food: herbivorous filter feeder

Reproduction: spawning takes place in tributary streams and along lakeshores in early summer; schooling adults release eggs in open water without regard to mates

Average Size: 6 to 8 inches, 1 to 8 ounces

Records: state—none; North American—4 pounds, 12 ounces, Lake Oahe, South Dakota, 2006

Notes: The Gizzard Shad is a widespread, prolific fish that is best known as forage for popular game fish. It can overpopulate some reservoirs and become the dominant species, growing too large to be prey for all but the largest game fish. The name "gizzard" refers to this shad's long, convoluted intestine that is often packed with sand. Though Gizzard Shad are a management problem at times, they form a valuable link in turning plankton into usable forage for larger game fish. Occasionally larger Gizzard Shad are caught with hook and line, but they have little food value.

Description: deep, laterally compressed silver body; dark olive back; several spots on shoulder behind the gill; head and cheeks bronze; sharply pointed scales along belly; more angular appearance than other shad.

Similar Species: American Shad (pg. 56), Gizzard Shad (pg. 58), Blueback Herring (pg. 54)

Hickory Shad

lower jaw does not extend beyond eye

American Shad

lower jaw extends beyond eye

Gizzard Shad

lower jaw does not extend beyond eye

Hickory Shad

multiple spots behind gill

Blueback Herring

single spot behind gill

Clupeidae

HICKORY SHAD
Alosa mediocris

Other Names: silver or bronze shad

Habitat: coastal marine most of the year; migrates up rivers and streams to spawn

Range: Atlantic coast from Maine to the St. Johns River in Florida and associated spawning rivers; Georgia—coastal and large Atlantic tributaries

Food: marine plankton feeder

Reproduction: Hickory Shad are anadromous, migrating to fresh water to spawn; spawning takes place at night when water temperatures reach 61 degrees; buoyant eggs are released and drift downstream with the current

Average Size: 10 to 14 inches, 1 pound to 1 pound, 8 ounces

Records: state—1 pound, 15 ounces, Ogeechee River, 1995; North American—2 pounds, 8 ounces, James River, Virginia 2006 (IGFA)

Notes: The Hickory Shad and the American Shad are the two large shad species that enter Georgia's coastal streams in the spring. Unlike American Shad, which prefer the main river currents, Hickory Shad prefer spawning in small tributary streams. The Hickory Shad is prized by light-tackle anglers for its strong fighting ability and high leaps when hooked. However, Hickory Shad are not as meaty as American Shad and not as popular for the table.

61

Description: silvery-yellow back with white sides and belly; dark spot on shoulder behind gill; deep laterally compressed body; small terminal mouth; last rays of dorsal fin form a long thread

Similar Species: Gizzard Shad (pg. 58)

Threadfin Shad	**Gizzard Shad**	**Threadfin Shad**	**Gizzard Shad**
terminal mouth	snout protrudes over mouth	yellow tail	no yellow on tail

THREADFIN SHAD

Clupeidae

Dorosoma petenense

Other Names: silver, yellow or thread shad

Habitat: currents of warm, large rivers and reservoirs; brackish and saline waters in coastal areas

Range: southern Mississippi River drainage through the Gulf States south into Central America; Georgia—scattered statewide in large bodies of water

Food: herbivorous filter feeder

Reproduction: schools of shad spawn in the shallows along shore when water temperatures reach the low 70s; adhesive eggs are spread over vegetation and left unguarded

Average Size: 2 to 5 inches

Records: none

Notes: The Threadfin Shad is similar to the Gizzard Shad but it is smaller and prefers currents in rivers and more open water in reservoirs. It is a southern species that has spread into the central US since the 1950s. Threadfin Shad are native in the Tennessee River drainage but have been stocked as forage for large game fish well beyond their native range. They require warm water and die when water temperatures drop below 41 degrees. When the water warms in summer, they migrate upstream and can become very abundant in some areas, but after cold winters they may be very scarce.

Description: silver body; reddish head and gills; dark tear-drop under eye; light star-shaped blotch on top of head; females have 6-8 black stripes; males have 11-15 vertical green bars

Similar Species: Brook Silverside (pg. 124), Mosquitofish (pg. 72)

Lined Topminnow	**Brook Silverside**	**Mosquitofish**
rounded anal fin	long anal fin with straight or concave edge	squared anal fin in females, long and pointed in males

Lined Topminnow	**Brook Silverside**	**Mosquitofish**
single dorsal fin	two dorsal fins	single dorsal fin

LINED TOPMINNOW

Fundulus lineolatus

Fundulidae

Other Names: starhead minnow, barred topminnow

Habitat: still pools in slow-moving streams; sandbars in freshwater lakes

Range: Atlantic and Gulf Coastal plains from Virginia to south Florida; Georgia—southeastern third of the state

Food: insects and crustaceans

Reproduction: spawns in late spring; eggs are spread in long filaments and are spread over shallow vegetation

Average Size: 1 to 2 inches

Records: none

Notes: Topminnows are also known as killifish. They inhabit the upper water column and are adapted to feeding on or near the surface. Though inconspicuous and well camou-flaged, they are the favorite targets of wading birds. The Lined Topminnow is common and can be very abundant in small ponds and backwater pools in Georgia's coastal plains and through the Okefenokee Swamp. They are hardy fish and are often used as bait minnows. The topminnows are not very colorful but make good aquarium fish, readily eat-ing food spread on the water's surface.

AMERICAN BROOK LAMPREY

CHESTNUT LAMPREY

Description: eel-like body; round, sucking-disk mouth; seven paired gill openings; long dorsal fin, extending to tail; no paired fins

Similar Species: American Eel (pg. 46), Sea Lamprey (pg. 68)

Freshwater Lampreys	**American Eel**	**Freshwater Lampreys**	**Sea Lamprey**
mouth is a sucking disk	mouth has jaws	undivided dorsal fin	dorsal divided by deep notch

FRESHWATER LAMPREYS

Ichthyomyzon, Lampetra

Petromyzontidae

Other Species: Least, Mountain and Gulf Brook Lampreys, Ohio Lamprey

Habitat: juveniles live in the quiet pools of streams and rivers; adults may move into some lakes

Range: Mississippi and Ohio River drainages in central US; Georgia—northern mountains

Food: juvenile lampreys are bottom dwellers and filter feeders in streams; adults are either parasitic on fish or do not feed

Reproduction: adults build nest in the gravel of streambeds when water temperatures reach the mid-50s; adults die soon after spawning

Average Size: 6 to 12 inches

Records: none

Notes: Lampreys are some of earth's oldest vertebrates, with fossil records dating back 500 million years. Georgia is home to six freshwater lamprey species; all are filter feeders for several years before they mature to adults. The Ohio and Chestnut Lampreys are parasitic in the adult form, often leaving small round wounds on their prey. The Brook Lampreys are non-parasitic and do not feed as adults. Georgia's native lampreys coexist with the other Georgia fish species with little or no effect on their populations. Due to deteriorating water conditions, many native lampreys are endangered or threatened throughout their range.

Description: eel-like body; round, sucking-disk mouth; seven paired gill openings; long dorsal fin extends to tail and is divided into two parts by a deep notch; no paired fins

Similar Species: Freshwater Lampreys (pg. 66), American Eel (pg. 46)

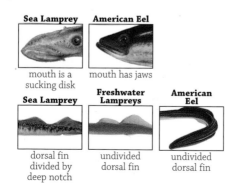

Sea Lamprey

mouth is a sucking disk

American Eel

mouth has jaws

Sea Lamprey

dorsal fin divided by deep notch

Freshwater Lampreys

undivided dorsal fin

American Eel

undivided dorsal fin

SEA LAMPREY
Petromyzon marinus

Other Names: landlocked or lake lamprey

Habitat: juveniles live in quiet pools of freshwater streams; adults are free-swimming in lakes or oceans

Range: Atlantic Ocean from Greenland to Florida, Norway to the Mediterranean; Georgia—coastal streams and a few impoundments

Food: juveniles are filter feeders in freshwater streams; adults are parasitic and attach to fish with a disk-shaped sucker mouth, then use their sharp tongue to rasp through the scales and feed on blood and bodily fluids; many "host" fish die

Reproduction: adults build a nest in the gravel of clear streams, then die shortly after spawning; young remain in the streams several years before returning to lakes or the sea as adults

Average Size: 12 to 24 inches

Records: none

Notes: The Sea Lamprey is native to the eastern coastal streams of North America. With the completion of the Welland Canal in 1829, Sea Lampreys bypassed Niagara Falls and entered the Great Lakes, reaching Lake Michigan in 1936. There they had a devastating effect on native fish populations. The Sea Lamprey is native to the coastal waters of Georgia and has never been a major problem for fish populations, even in the few impoundments where it has become landlocked.

SOUTHERN FLOUNDER

SUMMER FLOUNDER

Description: flat, flounder-like body with eyes on top;
side with eyes is light to dark brown with light spots and
blotches that extend to fins; light-brown mottled fins; side
without eyes is creamy white without spots

Similar Species: Hogchoker (pg. 128)

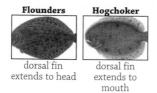

Flounders
dorsal fin
extends to head

Hogchoker
dorsal fin
extends to
mouth

SOUTHERN FLOUNDER
Paralichthys lethostigma

SUMMER FLOUNDER
Paralichthys dentatus

Other Names: mud flounder, doormat, halibut

Habitat: marine areas; migrates up freshwater rivers; prefers water with a sand or silt bottom

Range: the Atlantic coast from North Carolina to Florida, the Gulf Coast from Florida to Texas; Georgia—common in large coastal rivers

Food: small fish

Reproduction: adults migrate offshore to spawn in late fall

Average Size: 12 to 24 inches; 2 to 6 pounds

Records: state—none; North American—20 pounds, 9 ounces, Nassau Sound, Florida, 1982 (IGFA)

Notes: Flounders primarily inhabit the open ocean and estuaries, but many migrate into large freshwater rivers during the summer. Flounders are a common catch in the lower reaches of coastal rivers, but fishermen are often surprised when they catch one many miles from the ocean. Young flounders swim upright with an eye on each side; as they mature, one eye migrates, some to the left side and some to the right side. Southern and Summer Flounders belong to the family of left-eye flounders and the fish lie on their right side at maturity.

Description: silver to olive-green back and sides; scales out-lined giving sides a cross-hatched appearance; upturned mouth; dark bar under eye; rounded tail fin; males have a long pointed anal fin, females a small rounded anal fin

Similar Species: Brook Silverside (pg. 124), Lined Topminnow (pg. 64)

Mosquitofish	**Brook Silverside**	**Lined Topminnow**
squared anal fin in females, long and point-ed in males	long anal fin with straight or concave edge	rounded anal fin
Mosquitofish	**Brook Silverside**	**Lined Topminnow**
single dorsal fin	two dorsal fins	single dorsal fin

Poeciliidae

MOSQUITOFISH
Gambusia holbrooki

Other Names: mosquito or surface minnow

Habitat: surface of shallow, well-vegetated backwaters with little current; lakes and swamps

Range: the southeastern US; introduced worldwide; Georgia —primarily coastal lowlands, but possible statewide

Food: insects, crustaceans and some plant material

Reproduction: gives birth to live young after internal fertilization; may produce several broods in a single season

Average Size: 2 to 3 inches

Records: none

Notes: There are few native livebearers in the US, but it is a well-represented family in the tropical and subtropical Americas. Male Mosquitofish use their modified anal fin to transfer sperm to the much larger females. Females can then store the sperm for up to ten months. Mosquitofish have been introduced worldwide to control mosquitoes but seem to be no better at it than native species. Mosquitofish are hardy and can tolerate high temperatures, high salinity and low oxygen levels and can therefore be found in almost any quiet body of water.

BIGHEAD CARP

SILVER CARP

Description: low-set eyes; small body scales; no scales on head; large body; upturned mouth without barbels;

Similar Species: Common Carp (pg. 76), Grass Carp (pg. 78)

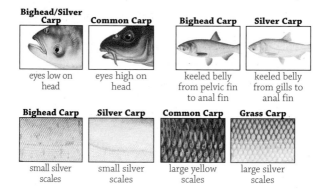

Bighead/Silver Carp	Common Carp
eyes low on head	eyes high on head

Bighead Carp	Silver Carp
keeled belly from pelvic fin to anal fin	keeled belly from gills to anal fin

Bighead Carp	Silver Carp	Common Carp	Grass Carp
small silver scales	small silver scales	large yellow scales	large silver scales

BIGHEAD CARP
Hypophthalmichthys nobilis

SILVER CARP *Hypophthalmichthys molitrix*

Other Names: Silver—shiner carp; Bighead—river carp, lake fish, speckled amur

Habitat: large, warm rivers and connected lakes

Range: native to Asia; introduced in other parts of the world; Georgia—restricted to aquaculture ponds

Food: plankton, algae

Reproduction: spawns from late spring to early summer in warm, flowing water

Average Size: 16 to 22 inches, 5 to 50 pounds

Records: state—none; North American—Bighead Carp, 90 pounds, Kirby Lake, Texas

Notes: Bighead and Silver Carp were introduced into the United States to control unwanted species in southern aquaculture ponds. They are important commercial fish farmed for food in many countries. Both species have escaped from ponds in Arkansas to become established in the Mississippi, Ohio and Illinois Rivers with devastating effect on native fish populations. Both species are voracious feeders that have the potential to disrupt the entire food web. Neither species is currently a problem in Georgia but they could become a threat to natural fish populations if they become established in the wild. If any are caught, they should not be returned to the water, and they should be killed, frozen, and given to a representative of the DNR.

Description: brassy yellow to golden brown or dark olive back and sides; white to yellow belly; two pairs of barbels near round, extendable mouth; red-tinged tail and anal fin; each scale has a dark spot at base and a dark margin

Similar Species: Grass Carp (pg. 78)

Common Carp

downturned mouth with barbels, eyes high on head

Grass Carp

upturned mouth lacks barbels, eyes low on head

COMMON CARP

Cyprinus carpio

Cyprinidae

Other Names: German, European, mirror or leather carp, buglemouth

Habitat: warm, shallow, quiet, weedy waters of streams and lakes

Range: native to Asia, introduced worldwide; Georgia— common statewide

Food: opportunistic feeder, prefers insect larvae, crustaceans and mollusks, but will eat algae and some higher plants

Reproduction: spawns from late spring to early summer in very shallow water at stream and lake edges; very obvious when spawning with a great deal of splashing

Average Size: 16 to 18 inches, 5 to 20 pounds

Records: state—35 pounds, 12 ounces, Lake Jackson, 1972; North American—57 pounds, 13 ounces, Tidal Basin, Washington, D.C., 1983

Notes: One of the world's most important freshwater species, the fast-growing Common Carp provides sport and food for millions of people throughout its range. This Asian minnow was introduced into Europe in the twelfth century but didn't make it to North America until the 1800s. Carp are a highly prized sport fish in Europe but are generally disliked in the US, even though Carp fight hard and have a fine flavor when taken from clean water. The meat is oily and bony and is best prepared by soaking it in a sweet brine and then smoking it.

Description: silver-gray head and sides with a golden-green sheen; fins grayish-green; large scales; eye set in middle of head, terminal mouth; torpedo-shaped body not as deep as common carp

Similar Species: Common Carp (pg. 76)

Grass Carp	Common Carp
mouth upturned, no barbels, eye low on head	downturned mouth with barbels, eye high on head

GRASS CARP

Ctenopharyngodon idella

Other Names: white amur, silver or weed carp

Habitat: warm, shallow, quiet, weedy waters of streams and lakes

Range: native to Siberia's lower Amur River and northern China, now established in 20 countries; Georgia—scattered ponds and impoundments throughout state

Food: aquatic vegetation

Reproduction: spawns in streams where eggs are released and fertilized in a slow current; only stocked as non-reproducing, sterile fish

Average Size: 24 to 30 inches, 5 to 20 pounds

Records: state—none; North American—80 pounds, Lake Wedington, Arkansas, 2004 (IGFA)

Notes: Grass Carp were first brought to the United States in 1961 by the US Fish and Wildlife Service to control aquatic vegetation. It was soon learned that by exposing the eggs to heat, sterile fish could be produced. These triploid fish (fish with three sets of chromosomes instead of the normal two) are now stocked in Georgia in order to control aquatic vegetation. A few have escaped to nearby streams. Grass Carp do not take bait readily, but a few are caught by anglers and are often large enough to put up a great fight. Grass Carp caught in posted vegetation control areas should be released so they can go about their job of weed control. In natural waters they should be removed.

FERAL GOLDFISH

RELEASED GOLDFISH

Description: color is variable; goldfish can be green, red, orange, gold, pink, or a variegated black and orange; deep body, fins heavy and rounded, dorsal fin originates just above or behind pectoral fins

Similar Species: Common Carp (pg. 76)

Goldfish	Common Carp	Goldfish	Common Carp
no chin barbels	chin barbels	dorsal fin originates just above or behind pelvic fins	dorsal fin originates just ahead of pelvic fins

Cyprinidae

GOLDFISH

Carassius auratus

Other Names: Golden Carp, Indiana, Baltimore or Missouri minnow

Habitat: quiet, well-vegetated stream pools; weedy lake edges

Range: native to Asia, introduced throughout the world, central US from coast to coast; Georgia—possible statewide

Food: scavenges both plant and animal matter

Reproduction: long spawning season from late spring through summer; spawns in very shallow water at stream and lake edges; very sticky eggs are spread over vegetation; no parental care

Average Size: 3 to 10 inches

Records: state—none; North American—3 pounds, 2 ounces, Lourdes Pond, Indiana, 2002

Notes: This exotic fish was first kept in hatcheries in the late 1800s and has become established in scattered locations throughout much of the US. Goldfish can become very common locally but infrequently become abundant enough to be much of a problem. There are few established populations in Georgia, but with frequent pet and bait releases they could be encountered. Goldfish frequently hybridize with Common Carp and through a unique fertilization process sometimes form all-female populations. The brightly colored fish are very susceptible to predation, thus established populations are predominately olive-green in color.

Description: dark olive back; silver-gray sides that reflect purple; large mouth; dark spot at base of dorsal fin; small barbel that fits in a groove between the back of the upper jaw and snout (very evident when the mouth is open)

Similar Species: Golden Shiner (pg. 88)

Creek Chub	Golden Shiner	Creek Chub	Golden Shiner
mouth large, extends to eye	small mouth barely extends to eye	rounded anal fin, 7 to 9 rays	angular anal fin, 11 to 15 rays

Cyprinidae

CREEK CHUB

Semotilus atromaculatus

Other Names: common, brook, silver, mud or blackspot chub, horned or northern horned dace

Habitat: primarily found in quiet pools in clear streams and rivers, occasionally in lakes

Range: Montana southeast through the Gulf States; Georgia—northern third of state

Food: small aquatic invertebrates and crustaceans

Reproduction: in late spring, male excavates a 1- to 3-foot long, teardrop-shaped pit at the head of stream riffles; using its mouth or rolling stones with its head, male fills pit to 6 to 8 inches high; females lay eggs on the mound, which are then covered and defended by the male; several other species spawn on the mounds, occasionally resulting in hybridization

Average Size: 4 to 10 inches, up to 8 ounces

Records: none

Notes: The Creek Chub is one of the most common stream fishes in eastern North America. They take bait readily and children spending a day on the creek often fish for them. When water levels are low in late summer, the chub spawning mounds can be plentiful and quite evident, leaving many to speculate on their origin. Chubs are a highly prized bait minnow, and local populations can be easily depleted by overharvesting.

Description: silver-brown back; silver lower sides and belly; scattered black scales on sides; very small scales; females have black stripe from nose to tail, stripe is faded in males; breeding males have a rusty, orange belly

Similar Species: Golden Shiner (pg. 88)

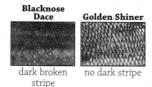

Blacknose Dace: dark broken stripe

Golden Shiner: no dark stripe

BLACKNOSE DACE

Rhinichthys atratulus

Other Names: striped or redfin dace, brook or potbelly minnow, slicker

Habitat: pools and runs of small to medium streams with a rock or gravel bottom

Range: Many drainages, including the Atlantic, Great Lakes, Hudson Bay, upper Mississippi and upper Mobile Bay drainages; Georgia—northern highlands

Food: small aquatic invertebrates

Reproduction: spawns in shallow water in late spring to early summer; groups of males gather over gravel, defending small territories with great flourish; eggs deposited in gravel left unattended

Average Size: $1^1/_2$ to 2 inches

Records: none

Notes: A small group of minnows in the US are referred to as daces. They are small fish that live in a variety of habitats but are most common in headwater streams. There are only a few dace species in Georgia; the Blacknose Dace is the most common and abundant. Female and non-breeding males are attractive, but unspectacular, in coloration. Breeding males develop a rusty red belly and are very attractive. Often found in large schools when streams are low, daces are very susceptible to overharvesting for bait.

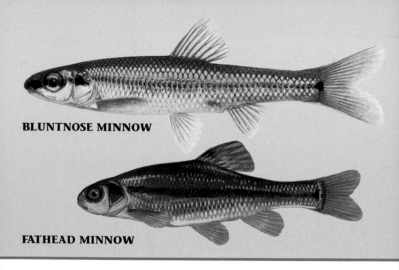

BLUNTNOSE MINNOW

FATHEAD MINNOW

Description: Bluntnose—yellow-brown back; silver sides with a cross-hatched appearance; dusky line from snout to tail, ending in a dark spot; Fathead—olive back; golden-yellow sides without cross-hatching; faded line from gills to tail (bright in breeding males), ending in a dark spot

Similar Species: Creek Chub (pg. 82)

Minnows	**Creek Chub**	**Bluntnose Minnow**	**Fathead Minnow**
small down-turned mouth	mouth large and terminal	mouth horizontal, overhung by snout	mouth oblique, not overhung by snout

Cyprinidae

BLUNTNOSE MINNOW
Pimephales notatus

FATHEAD MINNOW *Pimephales promelas*

Other Names: spottail minnow, tuffy

Habitat: shallow pools of small to midsized streams; shallow, weedy lakes and ponds

Range: central US from the Gulf to the Great Lakes; Georgia—southern two-thirds of the state

Food: insects and copepods

Reproduction: males prepare a nest beneath rocks and sticks; females enter nest and turn upside down to lay adhesive eggs on an overhang; male fans the eggs and massages them with a special mucus-like pad on his back

Average Size: 3 to 4 inches

Records: none

Notes: There are over 1,500 minnow species in the world, with 200 present in North America and over 90 species found in Georgia. The Bluntnose and Fathead Minnows are the most common bait pail minnows and are farmed throughout the Southeast. Without question, these are two of the most economically important fish in the US. The Bluntnose Minnow is not a native fish, whereas the Fathead may have been native in northern Georgia. Both species are now very abundant in some locations and small populations can be expected anywhere in Georgia because of escapees or bait pail releases.

GOLDEN SHINER

COMMON SHINER

Description: back gold to greenish-gold; sides golden with silver reflections; belly yellowish-silver; deep slab-sided body; mouth angled up; long, triangular head; lateral line has a very pronounced downward curve, with its lowest point just above the pelvic fins.

Similar Species: Creek Chub (pg. 82), Common Shiner

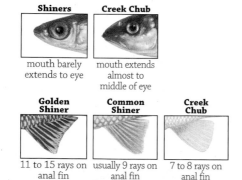

Shiners

mouth barely extends to eye

Creek Chub

mouth extends almost to middle of eye

Golden Shiner

11 to 15 rays on anal fin

Common Shiner

usually 9 rays on anal fin

Creek Chub

7 to 8 rays on anal fin

GOLDEN SHINER

Cyprinidae

Notemigonus crysoleucas

Other Names: bream, American bream, roach, American roach, butterfish, pond shiner

Habitat: clear, weedy ponds and quiet streams

Range: native to the eastern US south to Florida, introduced in the West; Georgia—possible statewide

Food: plankton, crustaceans, aquatic insects, mollusks

Reproduction: extended midsummer spawning season; a female attended by one or two males spreads adhesive eggs over submerged vegetation; no parental care

Average Size: 3 to 7 inches

Records: none

Notes: There are almost 40 Georgia minnows called shiners. Not all shiners are as flashy as the name indicates; some are dull and show almost no bright colors on their sides. The Golden Shiner is native to the streams in Georgia but is now frequently found in lakes. The Golden Shiner is a large, showy minnow that often congregates in large schools, particularly when young. Sometimes they feed in open water, but they are never far from vegetation. Both Golden and Common Shiners are important forage species and are now widely propagated and sold for bait. In Georgia, the Golden Shiner is the preferred large bait minnow, and they may be encountered in almost any stream or lake because of releases.

Description: olive-green back; tan to yellow-brown sides with faint, wavy vertical bars; rounded tail fin; dark bar just before the tail; slightly flattened head

Similar Species: Swampfish (pg. 42)

Eastern Mudminnow
jaws about even

Swampfish
lower jaw protrudes beyond snout

Eastern Mudminnow
solid color on sides, pelvic fins

Swampfish
bicolored, no pelvic fins

EASTERN MUDMINNOW

Umbra pygmaea

Umbridae

Other Names: coastal mudminnow, dogfish, mudfish

Habitat: large river backwaters; slow, stagnant waters of weedy streams and ponds with soft bottoms

Range: Atlantic states from New York to northern Florida; Georgia—east-central lowlands

Food: insects, mollusks and larger crustaceans

Reproduction: in the early spring, adults move into flooded pools when water temperatures reach the mid-50s; yellow-orange eggs are deposited singly on plant leaves and are left to hatch without parental care

Average Size: 3 inches

Records: none

Notes: This hardy little fish can withstand very low oxygen levels by gulping air to breathe when necessary (even from air bubbles under the ice). Eastern Mudminnows hide in the bottom detritus, but they do not bury themselves tail-first in the mud, as often reported. They are frequently the only fish left after ponds dry up and are depleted of oxygen. Not surprisingly, they are a good baitfish, withstanding the bait pail and hooks well. They can be fun aquarium fish and quickly learn to eat small pieces of meat or angleworms when offered.

91

Description: pale brown to sandy back and sides; sides are "tessellated," having a mosaic-like checkered pattern; markings become much more pronounced and colors are brighter on breeding males

Similar Species: Mottled Sculpin (pg. 122)

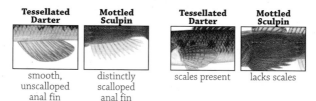

Tessellated Darter	Mottled Sculpin	Tessellated Darter	Mottled Sculpin
smooth, unscalloped anal fin	distinctly scalloped anal fin	scales present	lacks scales

TESSELLATED DARTER

Etheostoma olmstedi

Other Names: red-sided, yellowbelly, or weed darter

Habitat: the bottom of sandy, muddy pools of headwaters, creeks and small to medium rivers; lakeshore

Range: the Atlantic slope from the St. Lawrence River in Quebec to the St. Johns River in Florida; Georgia—east-central lowlands

Food: small aquatic invertebrates

Reproduction: in May and June, males migrate to shorelines or current edges to establish breeding areas; females move from territory to territory, spawning with several males; each sequence produces 7 to 10 eggs which attach to the bottom and are left without parental care

Average Size: 2 to 4 inches

Records: none

Notes: Relatives of the Yellow Perch and the Walleye, Darters are primarily stream fish and have adapted to living among the rocks in fast current. A small swim bladder allows Darters to sink rapidly to the bottom after a "dart," thereby avoiding being swept away by the current. Darters are hard to see when they move, but are easy to spot when perched on their pectoral fins. Georgia has a large number of darter species, many with very restricted ranges. The Tessellated Darter is one of the more common and widespread darters found in Georgia. Though the Tessellated Darter is primarily a stream species, it can be found in a wide range of habitats.

93

Description: back yellowish-brown to olive; sides lighter with 15 to 25 dark vertical bands; prominent dark spot at base of tail; pointed snout; long cylindrical body

Similar Species: Tessellated Darter (pg. 92)

Logperch	Tessellated Darter	Logperch	Tessellated Darter
larger mouth overhung by conical snout	small mouth, blunt nose	dorsal fins slightly separated	dorsal fins obviously separated

LOGPERCH

Percina carprodes

Other Names: Log or Manitou Darter, zebra fish, rock fish

Habitat: medium to large streams and rivers and large lakes

Range: Saskatchewan and Quebec, through the Great Lake states into the central US to the Gulf; Georgia—northeast corner of the state

Food: small aquatic invertebrates and algae

Reproduction: in late spring, adults move to the shallows; males form small mating schools (10 to 15 fish) that hover around a single female; adhesive eggs are deposited at random on sand; no parental care

Average Size: 3 to 6 inches

Records: none

Notes: The Logperch is the largest of the darters and is sometimes caught by anglers fishing stream edges or lake shorelines. When caught, they are frequently mistaken for small perch or walleye. The name refers to their habit of floating motionless in cover like small logs. With increased pollution, many Georgia Logperch populations have been negatively impacted, and this is true in other states as well. Logperch are common forage for game fish but are not hardy enough to be a good baitfish. However, they are showy and active and make good aquarium fish.

Description: slender body; gray to dark silver or yellowish-brown with dark blotches on sides; black spots on spiny dorsal fin; may exhibit some white on lower margin of tail, but lacks the prominent white spot found on the Walleye

Similar Species: Walleye (pg. 98)

Sauger	Walleye	Sauger	Walleye
spiny dorsal fin is spotted, lacks dark blotch on rear base	spiny dorsal fin lacks spots, large dark blotch on rear base	blotches on sides below lateral line	lacks blotches on sides below lateral line

SAUGER

Sander canadensis

Other Names: sand pike, spotfin pike, river pike, jackfish, jack salmon

Habitat: large lakes and rivers

Range: large lakes in southern Canada, the northern US and the wider reaches of the Mississippi, Missouri, Ohio and Tennessee River drainages; Georgia—native to Tennessee River drainage

Food: small fish, aquatic insects, crayfish

Reproduction: spawns in April and May as water approaches 50 degrees; adults move into the shallow waters of tributaries and headwaters to randomly deposit eggs over gravel beds

Average Size: 10 to 12 inches, 8 ounces to 2 pounds

Records: state—4 pounds, 3 ounces, Clarks Hill Lake, 1986; North American—8 pounds, 12 ounces, Lake Sakakawea, North Dakota, 1971

Notes: Though the Sauger is the Walleye's smaller cousin, it is a big-water fish, residing primarily in large lakes and rivers. It grows slowly, and only reaches two pounds after twenty years in very cold water. The Sauger is native to the Tennessee drainage but was not originally found east of the Appalachians. It is an aggressive daytime feeder when compared to Walleye, but is still more productively fished in the evenings, early mornings and at night. Its fine, flavored flesh is top table fare.

Description: long, round body; dark silver or golden to dark olive-brown sides; spines in both first dorsal and anal fins; sharp canine teeth; dark spot at base of the last three spines of the dorsal fin; white spot on bottom lobe of tail

Similar Species: Sauger (pg. 96)

Walleye

spiny dorsal fin lacks spots, large dark blotch on rear base

Sauger

spiny dorsal fin is spotted, lacks dark blotch on rear base

Walleye

lacks blotches on sides below lateral line

Sauger

blotches on sides below lateral line

WALLEYE
Sander vitreus

Other Names: marble-eyes, walleyed pike, jack, jackfish, Susquehanna salmon

Habitat: lakes and streams, abundant in very large lakes

Range: originally the northern states and Canada, now widely stocked throughout the US; Georgia—stocked in a few rivers and reservoirs across state

Food: mainly small fish, but also eats insects, crayfish and leeches

Reproduction: spawns in tributary streams or rocky lake shoals when spring water temperatures reach 45 to 50 degrees; no parental care

Average Size: 14 to 17 inches, 1 to 3 pounds

Records: state—11 pounds, 6 ounces, Richard B. Russell Lake, 1995; North American—21 pounds, 11 ounces, Greer's Ferry Lake, Arkansas, 1982

Notes: Walleyes are revered by anglers everywhere, and are the most popular sport fish in many northern states. Walleyes are not strong fighters, but are considered one of the best eating freshwater fish. A reflective layer of pigment in its eye allows it to see in low-light conditions. As a result, Walleyes are most active at dusk, dawn and throughout the night and during other low-light conditions, such as overcast skies and beneath waves sometimes called "Walleye chop." Native to the Tennessee drainage, they were rare in Georgia until recent stocking programs produced a strong population for sport fishing.

Description: 6 to 9 olive-green vertical bars on a yellow-brown background; two separate dorsal fins, the front all spines, the back soft rays; lower fins are tinged yellow-orange, brighter in breeding males

Similar Species: Sauger (pg. 96), Walleye (pg. 98)

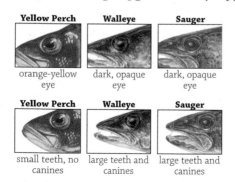

Yellow Perch	**Walleye**	**Sauger**
orange-yellow eye	dark, opaque eye	dark, opaque eye

Yellow Perch	**Walleye**	**Sauger**
small teeth, no canines	large teeth and canines	large teeth and canines

YELLOW PERCH

Perca flavescens

Other Names: ringed, striped or jack perch, green hornet

Habitat: lakes and streams; prefers clear, open water

Range: widely introduced throughout southern Canada and the northern US; Georgia—introduced to lowland rivers and some lakes

Food: prefers minnows, insects, snails, leeches and crayfish

Reproduction: spawns at night in shallow, weedy areas when water temperatures reach 45 degrees; females drape gelatinous ribbons of eggs on submerged vegetation

Average Size: 8 to 11 inches, 6 to 10 ounces

Records: state—2 pounds, 8 ounces, Lake Burton, 1980; North American—4 pounds, 3 ounces, Bordentown, New Jersey, 1865

Notes: The Yellow Perch is very common throughout much of the United States and has been introduced far beyond its native range. Over much of its range it is a popular panfish; there is even a commercial fishery in the Great Lakes. In Georgia, Yellow Perch can be very abundant locally, but they are often stunted and quite small. A few Georgia anglers consider perch their primary panfish. When perch are large enough to keep, they have firm, white flesh and are excellent table fare. Many anglers in northern states rank Yellow Perch alongside Walleye in terms of flavor.

Description: olive-green to yellow-brown back and sides; yellow-green chain-like markings on the sides; distinct dark teardrop below the eye; scales on the entire cheek and gill covers; fins almost clear

Similar Species: Redfin Pickerel (pg. 104), Grass Pickerel (pg. 104), Northern Pike (pg. 108)

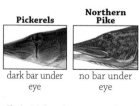

Pickerels	**Northern Pike**
dark bar under eye	no bar under eye

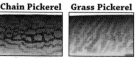

Chain Pickerel	**Grass Pickerel**	**Redfin Pickerel**
chain-like marks on sides	lacks distinct chain marks	lacks distinct chain marks

CHAIN PICKEREL

Esocidae

Esox niger

Other Names: weed, jack or chain pike, jack pickerel

Habitat: shallow, weedy lakes and sluggish streams

Range: the eastern United States from the Great Lakes and Maine to Florida and west through the Gulf States to Texas; Georgia—statewide except in the mountains

Food: small fish, aquatic invertebrates

Reproduction: spawning takes place in April and May just as the water begins to warm; adhesive eggs are deposited over shallow submerged vegetation and left to hatch with no parental care; occasionally spawns in fall with very low survival rate

Average Size: 18 to 24 inches, 1 to 3 pounds

Records: state—9 pounds, 6 ounces, Homerville, 1961; North American—9 pounds, 6 ounces; Homerville, Georgia, 1961

Notes: The Chain Pickerel is the largest of the pickerels and a respected game fish. Chain Pickerels frequent the outside edges of weedbeds and bite readily on minnow imitation lures. When fished on light tackle or a fly rod, they put up a good fight. Chain Pickerels have a tendency to stunt when overpopulated, filling lakes and channels with half-pound "hammer handles". All members of the pike family have intramuscular "Y" bones, an adaptation which enables them to lunge suddenly to capture prey. The Chain Pickerel's flesh is flavorful, but their small "Y" bones make them unpopular as table fare.

GRASS PICKEREL

REDFIN PICKEREL

Description: both fish—olive-green to yellow-brown back and sides; distinct dark bar below eye that slopes back; scales on entire cheek and gill cover; Grass Pickerel—distinct wavy bars on sides; lower fins cream-colored; Redfin Pickerel—indistinct wavy bars on side; lower fins red (bright in breeding males)

Similar Species: Chain Pickerel (pg. 102), Northern Pike (pg. 108)

Redfin/Grass Pickerel

bar under eye slopes back

Chain Pickerel

vertical bar under eye

Northern Pike

no bar under eye

Redfin Pickerel

up to three notched scales between pelvic fins

Grass Pickerel

more than six notched scales between pelvic fins

GRASS PICKEREL

Esox americanus vermiculatus

REDFIN PICKEREL *Esox americanus americanus*

Species Names: red, mud, banded or little pickerel, red, grass, red-finned or mud pike

Habitat: shallow, weedy lakes and sluggish streams

Range: Atlantic states from Maine to Florida (Redfins east of the Alleghenies, Grass west of Alleghenies) and east through the Gulf States; Georgia—statewide south of the mountains

Food: small fish, aquatic invertebrates

Reproduction: both enter flooded meadows and shallow bays to spawn in early spring; adhesive eggs are deposited over submerged vegetation and left to hatch with no parental care

Average Size: 10 to 12 inches, under 1 pound

Records: state (Redfin)—2 pounds, 10 ounces, Lewis Lake, 1982; North American—2 pounds, 10 ounces, Lewis Lake, Georgia, 1982

Notes: The Redfin and the Grass Pickerel are varieties of the same fish. These pickerels are the smallest member of the pike family and are commonly found in weedy lakes and streams in Georgia. Redfin and Grass Pickerels eat some small fish but their diet consists largely of invertebrates, including crayfish. Redfin Pickerels are scrappy fighters on light tackle, but due to their small size are little more than a nuisance to panfish anglers.

105

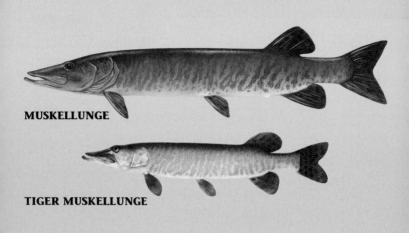

MUSKELLUNGE

TIGER MUSKELLUNGE

Description: torpedo-shaped body; dorsal fin near tail; dark gray-green back; silver to silver-green sides; dark vertical bars or blotches on sides (dark markings on light background); pointed tail; no scales on lower half of gill covers

Similar Species: Chain Pickerel (pg. 102), Northern Pike (pg. 108)

Muskellunge	Chain Pickerel	Northern Pike
dark marks on light background	chain-like marks on sides	light marks on dark background

Muskellunge	Northern Pike	Tiger Muskellunge
pointed tail	rounded tail	rounded tail

MUSKELLUNGE

Esocidae

Esox masquinongy

Other Names: Great Lakes or Ohio Muskellunge, muskie, northern, 'ski, 'lunge

Habitat: waters of large, clear, weedy lakes; medium to large rivers with slow currents and deep pools

Range: the Great Lakes basin east to Maine, south through the Ohio River drainage to Tennessee; Georgia—stocked in several rivers and lakes across the state

Food: small fish; occasionally baby muskrats, ducklings

Reproduction: spawning takes place in late spring when water temperatures reach 50 to 60 degrees; eggs are laid in dead vegetation in streams or bays with a soft bottom

Average Size: 30 to 42 inches, 10 to 20 pounds

Records: state—38 pounds, Lake Blue Ridge, 1957; North American—69 pounds, 11 ounces, Chippewa Flowage, Wisconsin, 1949

Notes: The Muskellunge is the prize of all freshwater game fishing. This big, fast predator prefers large, shallow, clear lakes or rivers with quiet pools. They are hard to entice with lures or bait and muskie fishermen average over 50 hours of fishing before catching a legal fish. Muskellunge readily hybridize with Northern Pike, producing Tiger Muskellunge, and pure musky stock is rare in many natural populations. Tiger Muskellunge are easier to rear and preferred for many stocking programs. Muskies are northern fish and are not native to Georgia but are now stocked in some lakes.

Description: elongated body with dorsal fin near tail; head long and flattened in front, forming a duck-like snout; dark green back; light green sides with bean-shaped light spots (light markings on dark background)

Similar Species: Muskellunge (pg. 106), Chain Pickerel (pg. 102)

Northern Pike	**Chain Pickerel**	**Muskellunge**
light spots on dark background	chain-like marks on sides	dark marks on light background

Northern Pike	**Muskellunge**
rounded tail	pointed tail

NORTHERN PIKE

Esox lucius

Other Names: northern, pickerel or great northern pickerel, jack or jackfish, hammer handle, snot rocket

Habitat: lakes and slow-moving streams often associated with vegetation

Range: northern Europe, Asia and North America; Georgia—stocked in a few lakes across the state

Food: small fish, frogs, crayfish

Reproduction: in early spring as water temperature reaches 34 to 40 degrees, eggs are laid among shallow vegetation in tributary streams and near lake edges; no parental care

Average Size: 18 to 24 inches, 2 to 5 pounds

Records: state—18 pounds, 2 ounces, Lake Rabun, 1982; North American—46 pounds, 2 ounces, Great Sacandaga Lake, New York, 1940

Notes: This large, fast predator is one of the most widespread freshwater fish in the world but is not native to Georgia. Its long, tube-shaped body and intramuscular bones are adaptations for quick bursts of speed. Pike are sight-feeders and hunt by lying in wait and capturing their prey with a lighting-fast lunge. Many anglers have lost their catch just at the boat when the pike employed this burst of speed to escape. The Tiger Muskie is a hybrid of a Northern Pike and a Muskellunge and is considered a Muskie in bag limits.

Description: dark green to gray-green back; lower sides dark tan with black specks; body has an overall purple sheen; dark bar at base of tail; single dorsal fin; big mouth and head; anus just below gills

Similar Species: Fathead Minnow (pg. 86)

Pirate Perch

protruding
lower jaw

Fathead Minnow

snout protrudes
over mouth

Pirate Perch

slight notch
in tail

Fathead Minnow

deep notch
in tail

PIRATE PERCH

Aphredoderus sayanus

Other Names: green perch

Habitat: low gradient streams and creeks, swamps, ponds and roadside ditches, all with a soft bottom and thick vegetation

Range: the Mississippi drainage to the Great Lakes; the Gulf and Atlantic states; Georgia—southern half

Food: insects, crustaceans and small fish

Reproduction: from early spring through summer, both adults build a nest then guard eggs and young

Average Size: 2 to 5 inches

Records: none

Notes: Pirate Perch are small, secretive fish that hide during the day in thick aquatic vegetation or bottom debris. They aggressively feed on insects during the early morning, late evening and at night. In juvenile fish, the anus is near the anal fins, but it migrates to the gill area as the fish matures. In other species, this trait is associated with eggs that are brooded under the gill covers; however, gill brooding has not been observed in Pirate Perch. Pirate Perch were named for their propensity to attack and kill other fish when kept in an aquarium. A few anglers feel this hardy little fish is superior to other baitfish and go to great lengths to obtain them.

Description: blue-gray back; silver-green sides with 5 to 8 triangular-shaped, dark gray-brown bars; deep body; protruding lip; breeding males have blue body with brassy cheeks, breast and belly and orange fins

Similar Species: Mosquitofish (pg. 72), Fathead/Bluntnose Minnows (pg. 86)

Sheepshead Minnow

squared tail

Bluntnose Minnow

deep notch in tail

Fathead Minnow

deep notch in tail

Mosquitofish

rounded tail

Sheepshead Minnow

rounded anal fin

Mosquitofish

pointed anal fin

SHEEPSHEAD MINNOW

Cyprinodon variegatus

Other Names: chubby, variegated minnow, sheepshead or broad killifish, sheepshead or Eustis pupfish

Habitat: quiet shallows of small streams or swamps with a muddy bottom; often found in open water near vegetation; frequents both fresh and brackish waters

Range: Maine to the Yucatan and Venezuela, the Bahamas; Georgia—coastal streams and lakes and a few inland waters

Food: plant material, algae, detritus and aquatic insects

Reproduction: in spring through early summer, males construct and defend nest in open sandy areas; females lay adhesive eggs that attach to plants or stick to open sand

Average Size: 2 to 3 inches

Records: none

Notes: The Sheepshead Minnow is more common in brackish water over much of its range, but in Georgia it can be very abundant locally in both fresh and brackish water. Sheepshead Minnows found in lakes are not as thick bodied as those found in brackish water and take on a much more elongated shape. This large, stout minnow is a popular aquarium fish and baitfish. Sheepshead Minnows are very hardy, even in marine conditions; they are one of the preferred baits when flounder fishing. When introduced to new habitats, Sheepshead Minnows readily hybridize with local pupfish species, often outcompeting and eliminating the native fish.

Description: dark olive-green to brown body and head covered with black specks; 10 or 11 black bands on sides; black bands on dorsal, anal and tail fins; sunfish shape with rounded fins

Similar Species: Pirate Perch (pg. 110), Warmouth (pg. 174), Sunfish (pp. 160-172)

Banded Pygmy Sunfish

pointed pelvic fins

Pirate Perch

rounded pelvic fins

Warmouth

rounded pelvic fins

Banded Pygmy Sunfish

hard rays not separated from soft rays

Sunfish (all)

hard rays distinct from soft rays

BANDED PYGMY SUNFISH

Elassoma zonatum

Other Names: little banded sunfish

Habitat: lakes, creeks and coastal swamps that are heavily vegetated with quiet waters and a soft bottom

Range: southeastern states from North Carolina to eastern Texas and the Mississippi Valley through the Ohio basin to southern Illinois; Georgia—southern half of the state

Food: aquatic insects, zooplankton

Reproduction: males guard small territories but do not build nests; eggs are laid in the vegetation and left with no parental care

Average Size: 1 to $1^1/_2$ inches

Records: none

Notes: Pygmy Sunfish are small, solitary fish that hide in dense vegetation and are most often seen when they enter minnow traps set near weedbeds. They look like tiny sunfish and were once thought to be a related species, though it has been determined that they are unrelated and have been placed in their own family. There are four Pygmy Sunfish species found in Georgia. The Banded Sunfish is the most common and widespread; the Everglades Sunfish is a close second. Both species can be very abundant. Pygmy Sunfish adapt well to aquariums and the Everglades Pygmy Sunfish has long been popular in the European pet trade.

Description: back varies from olive and blue-gray to black with worm-like markings; sides bronze to olive with red spots tinged light brown; lower fins red-orange with white leading edge; tail squared or slightly forked

Similar Species: Brown Trout (pg. 118), Rainbow Trout (pg. 120)

Brook Trout	**Brown Trout**	**Rainbow Trout**
worm-like marks, red spots	large dark spots, small red dots	pink stripe on silvery body

BROOK TROUT
Salvelinus fontinalis

Other Names: speckled, squaretail or coaster trout, brookie

Habitat: cool, clear streams and small lakes with moderate vegetation; prefers water temperatures of 50 to 60 degrees

Range: Great Lakes region north to Labrador, south through the Appalachians to Georgia, introduced widely; Georgia— throughout the mountain region

Food: insects, small fish, leeches, crustaceans

Reproduction: spawns in late fall when water temperature reaches 40 to 49 degrees; female builds 4- to 12-inch deep nest, then buries fertilized eggs in loose gravel; eggs hatch in 50 to 150 days

Average Size: 8 to 10 inches, eight ounces

Records: state—5 pounds, 10 ounces, Waters Creek, 1986; North American—14 pounds, 8 ounces, Nipigon River, Ontario, 1916

Notes: The Brook Trout is a beautiful fish native to the mountain streams of Georgia. Though there are still many wild populations of Brook Trout, they are not very tolerant of environmental change and many streams throughout their range can no longer support them. It is now common for native Brook Trout populations to be augmented with hatchery fish. Brook Trout have bright, orange flesh that is firm and has a delicate flavor prized by trout fishermen.

BROWN TROUT

TIGER TROUT

Description: golden brown to olive back and sides; large dark spots on sides, the dorsal fin and sometimes the upper lobe of tail; red spots with light halos scattered along sides

Similar Species: Brook Trout (pg. 116), Rainbow Trout (pg. 120)

Brown Trout	Brook Trout	Rainbow Trout
dark spots on brown or olive background	worm-like marks on back	pink stripe on silvery body

Salmonidae

BROWN TROUT

Salmo trutta

Other Names: German brown, Loch Leven or spotted trout

Habitat: open ocean near its spawning streams and clear, cold, gravel-bottomed streams; shallow portions of the Great Lakes

Range: Native to Europe from the Mediterranean to Siberia, introduced widely; Georgia—northern mountain streams

Food: insects, crayfish, small fish

Reproduction: spawns in headwater streams, tributaries and stream mouths when migration is blocked; female fans out a saucer-shaped nest that male guards until spawning; female covers eggs

Average Size: 11 to 20 inches, 2 to 6 pounds

Records: state—18 pounds, 6 ounces, Chattahoochee River, 2001; North American—40 pounds, 4 ounces, Little Red River, Arkansas, 1992

Notes: Brought to North America from Europe in the late 1800s, the Brown Trout were successfully stocked in Georgia in the early 1900s. In many states the introduced Brown Trout soon replaced the native Brook Trout and Georgia was no exception. Brown Trout prefer cold, clear streams, but will tolerate warmer water and turbidity better than other trout. Brown Trout are the favorite of fly fishermen around the world. It is a secretive and hard-to-catch species, and often feeds at night. Many states have rules restricting night trout fishing. Brown Trout occasionally hybridize with Brook Trout to produce the colorful, but sterile, Tiger Trout. **119**

Description: blue-green to brown head and back; silver lower sides with pink to rose stripe; entire body covered with small black spots; adipose fin

Similar Species: Brook Trout (pg. 116), Brown Trout (pg. 118)

Rainbow Trout

pink stripe on silvery body

Brown Trout

sides lack pink stripe

Rainbow Trout

lacks worm-like marks

Brook Trout

worm-like marks on back

RAINBOW TROUT

Salmonidae

Oncorhynchus mykiss

Other Names: steelhead, Pacific, Kamloops or silver trout

Habitat: prefers whitewater in cool streams and coastal regions of large lakes; tolerates smaller, cool, clear lakes

Range: the Pacific Ocean and coastal streams from Mexico to Alaska; introduced worldwide, Georgia—northern mountain streams and rivers

Food: insects, small crustaceans, fish

Reproduction: predominantly spring spawners but some fall spawning varieties exist; female builds nest in well-aerated gravel in both streams and lakes

Average Size: 20 to 22 inches, 1 to 2 pounds

Records: state—17 pounds, 8 ounces, Soque River, 2004; North American—42 pounds, 2 ounces, Bell Island, Alaska, 1970

Notes: This Pacific Trout was brought to Georgia in the late 1800s and was soon established in self-sustaining populations. However his heavily fished species is maintained in most waters only through continuous restocking. Even so, it is the most common, widespread and popular trout in Georgia. Rainbow Trout are more tolerant of poor water conditions than Brook Trout; some varieties can survive temperatures into the 80s for short periods. Steelhead Trout are Rainbow Trout that migrate from spawning streams into the open ocean or the Great Lakes as adults.

121

Description: slate-gray to blotchy olive-brown back; large mouth; eyes set almost on top of head; large, wing-like pectoral fins; no scales

Similar Species: Tessellated Darter (pg. 92)

Mottled Sculpin	Tessellated Darter
distinctly scalloped anal fin	smooth, unscalloped anal fin

Mottled Sculpin	Tessellated Darter
lacks scales	scales present

MOTTLED SCULPIN

Cottus bairdii

Other Names: common sculpin, muddler, gudgeon

Habitat: bottom dwellers of cool, swift, hard-bottomed streams or wave-swept lakeshores with rocks or vegetation

Range: eastern US through Canada to the Hudson Bay and the Rocky Mountains; Georgia—the northern mountains

Food: aquatic invertebrates, fish eggs, small fish

Reproduction: spawns in late spring when water temperature reaches 63 to 73 degrees; male builds a nest under ledges, logs or stream banks, then entices female with an elaborate courtship ritual; female turns upside down to deposit eggs on the "roof" of the nest; male attends to nest through hatching

Average Size: 4 to 5 inches

Records: none

Notes: Sculpins are cold-water fish, occupying mountain streams or deep, northern lakes. There are five sculpins found in Georgia, but some have very restricted ranges. The Mottled Sculpin is one of the most abundant. This stream fish inhabits the same waters as Rainbow and Brown Trout, though it can tolerate somewhat warmer conditions than either trout species. To a certain degree, Sculpins can modify their body color to blend in with the bottom. Mottled Sculpins are forage for many top predators and are a preferred bait when fishing for large Brown Trout.

123

Description: sides bright silver to silver-green with conspicuous light stripe; long, thin body; upturned mouth; 2 dorsal fins; tail deeply forked and pointed

Similar Species: Lined Topminnow (pg. 64), Mosquitofish (pg. 72)

Brook Silverside	**Lined Topminnow**	**Mosquitofish**
long anal fin with straight or concave edge	rounded anal fin	squared anal fin in females, fin is long and pointed in males
Brook Silverside	**Lined Topminnow**	**Mosquitofish**
two dorsal fins	single dorsal fin	single dorsal fin

BROOK SILVERSIDE

Labidesthes sicculus

Atherinidae

Other Names: northern silverside, skipjack, friar

Habitat: surface of clear lakes; slack water of large streams

Range: Great Lake states south through the central US to the Gulf States; Georgia—southern two-thirds of the state

Food: aquatic and flying insects

Reproduction: spawns in late spring and early summer; eggs are laid in sticky strings attached to vegetation; most adults die after spawning

Average Size: 3 to 4 inches

Records: none

Notes: The Brook Silverside is a member of a large family of primarily marine fish that live mostly in tropical and subtropical regions. It is a flashy fish that is often seen cruising near the surface in small schools. Its upturned mouth is an adaptation to surface feeding. It is not uncommon to see Brook Silversides make spectacular leaps from the water, flying-fish style, in pursuit of prey. The Silverside has a short lifespan, often lasting only 15 months.

Description: dark brown back fading to lighter brown sides with irregular blotches; large scales on head; large mouth with sharp teeth; long, single dorsal fin

Similar Species: Bowfin (pg. 24)

Northern Snakehead	Bowfin	Northern Snakehead	Bowfin
enlarged scales on head	no head scales, bony plates between jaws	pelvic fins near head, long anal fin	pelvic fins at mid-body, short anal fin

NORTHERN SNAKEHEAD

Channidae

Channa argus

Other Names: amur or ocellated snakehead, "frankenfish"

Habitat: stagnant, shallow ponds and slow-moving streams with a muddy or weedy bottom

Range: native to China and Korea; introduced to Japan, Eastern Europe and five US states; Georgia—not reported in state

Food: fish, crayfish, frogs

Reproduction: females can spawn several times a year beginning in June and lay 100,000 eggs

Average Size: 12 to 24 inches, 2 to 5 pounds

Records: none

Notes: Northern Snakeheads were brought to the US for live fish markets and as aquarium pets, and then they escaped or were released. Several Snakeheads have been found in the Carolinas and other eastern states. The species is not thought to be established in any of these states and has not been recorded in Georgia, where it is now illegal to possess live snakeheads. Snakeheads have a modified swim bladder that allows them to breathe air. They can slither through wet marshes for up to three days to reach new lakes. Snakeheads are voracious predators that can tolerate temperatures from freezing to near 90 degrees. This highly competitive invader has the potential to devastate native fish populations. Anglers should learn to identify Snakeheads; if any Snakeheads are caught, they should be killed, frozen and given to a conservation officer. **127**

Description: color variable, side with eyes is mottled light to dark brown or olive-green with 6 to 8 dark bands across the body; mottled fins; side without eyes is white; flat flounder-like body with eyes on top; tiny rough scales give body a hairy texture

Similar Species: Southern/Summer Flounders (pg. 70)

Hogchoker   **Flounders**

dorsal fin extends to mouth   dorsal and anal fins extend to head

HOGCHOKER

Trinectes maculatus

Other Names: hogchoker flounder

Habitat: marine areas; freshwater streams with open sand or silt bottom

Range: Atlantic coast from Massachusetts to Venezuela, Gulf Coast from Florida to Texas; Georgia—common in coastal rivers

Food: crustaceans and aquatic insects

Reproduction: in early summer, adults return to marine estuaries to spawn; after hatching, larvae migrate up freshwater streams to mature; a 6-inch female may contain over 50,000 eggs

Average Size: 4 to 6 inches

Records: none

Notes: Hogchokers are plentiful, coastal river fish that are most often encountered when caught in crab traps, fish traps or nets. Once caught, Hogchokers quickly attach themselves to nets, buckets and fishermen. For this reason, Hogchokers leave a lasting impression. Their spiny scales and feathery fins feel fuzzy when handled. Hogchokers were reportedly named because the fish lodged in pigs' throats after hogs were fed the commonly netted fish.

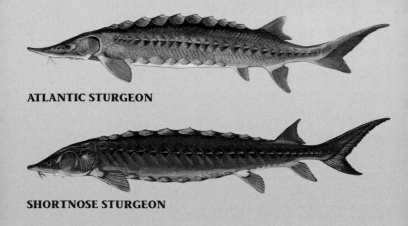

ATLANTIC STURGEON

SHORTNOSE STURGEON

Description: Atlantic—slate-gray back and sides; snout long with a narrow mouth; two rows of scutes (bony plates) before anus; Shortnose—dark brown to black back and sides; snout short with large, wide mouth; both species have five rows of scutes (bony plates), one on the back, two on the sides, two on the bottom; tail is shark-like with the upper lobe much longer than the lower

Similar Species: none

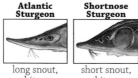

Atlantic Sturgeon	Shortnose Sturgeon
long snout, white on leading edge of paired fins	short snout, white on trailing edge of paired fins

130

ATLANTIC STURGEON

Acipenser oxyrhyncus

Acipenseridae

SHORTNOSE STURGEON *Acipenser brevirostrum*

Other Names: none

Habitat: large coastal rivers and estuaries

Range: Atlantic Sturgeon—Atlantic coast from Labrador to Florida, the Gulf Coast to the Mississippi River; Georgia—possible in any large coastal stream; Shortnose Sturgeon—Atlantic coast from New Brunswick to Central Florida; Georgia—coastal streams

Food: snails, clams, crayfish and insects

Reproduction: migrates to brackish estuaries or freshwater rivers to spawn; thousands of eggs are laid and fertilized a few at a time in the current of large rivers

Average Size: Atlantic—8 to 12 feet, 300 to 400 pounds; Shortnose—2 to 3 feet, 6 to 8 pounds

Records: none

Notes: Sturgeons are primitive fish with a long history. Once an important commercial fish harvested for both meat and caviar, both species are now either threatened or endangered. Shortnose Sturgeons are very rare and have only recently reappeared in many coastal waters. The Atlantic Sturgeon is not as rare and is still occasionally caught offshore and in larger rivers. Because of their shark-like tails, the sturgeon are often mistaken for sharks in coastal regions, but they have small toothless mouths. Any sightings should be reported to the DNR, and every attempt should be made to return a hooked fish to the water unharmed.

131

Description: slate-green back with bronze sides; large, dark eye; deep, laterally compressed body; rounded head; blunt snout; small downturned mouth with thick lips

Similar Species: Common Carp (pg. 76)

Smallmouth Buffalo	Common Carp
mouth lacks barbels	barbels below mouth

SMALLMOUTH BUFFALO

Ictiobus bubalus

Other Names: razorback, highback, humpback, or thick-lipped buffalo

Habitat: moderate to swift currents in the deep, clean waters of larger streams and some lakes

Range: the Missouri, Mississippi and Ohio River drainages south to the Gulf and west into New Mexico; Georgia—native to the Tennessee drainage in northeast Georgia; introduced in a few other streams and lakes

Food: small mollusks, aquatic insect larvae and zooplankton

Reproduction: spawns in clear, shallow water of flooded fields and marshes when water temperature reaches the low 60s; young quickly return to main streams when water recedes

Average Size: 18 to 20 inches, 10 to 12 pounds

Records: state—none; North American—73 pounds, 1 ounce; Lake Koshkonong, Wisconsin, 2004

Notes: There are three sucker species in North America called buffaloes; the Smallmouth Buffalo is the only species routinely found in Georgia. It requires deep, clean water and feeds heavily on aquatic insect larvae. The Smallmouth Buffalo is commercially harvested in many large rivers and is highly respected as table fare. The Smallmouth Buffalo is a powerful fighter and can be a challenge to land when hooked near fast current. Few Buffalo are taken by anglers, but they can be caught by using small insect baits floated near the bottom.

Description: olive-brown back and sides with a golden sheen; dark-edged scales on sides; creamy-white below lateral line; rounded edge on dorsal fin; stubby thick body; breeding males have 3 large tubercles on side of head; young have a yellow stripe above a black stripe that runs from mouth to tail

Similar Species: Northern Hog Sucker (pg. 140), Spotted Sucker (pg. 142)

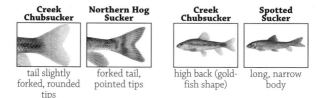

Creek Chubsucker	Northern Hog Sucker	Creek Chubsucker	Spotted Sucker
tail slightly forked, rounded tips	forked tail, pointed tips	high back (goldfish shape)	long, narrow body

Catostomidae

CREEK CHUBSUCKER

Erimyzon oblongus

Other Names: chubsucker, sweet or yellow sucker

Habitat: deep pools of clear, hard-bottomed creeks and small rivers with some vegetation; eastern lakes and reservoirs

Range: Atlantic slope drainages from Maine to Georgia; the Mississippi basin from the Great Lakes almost to Gulf Coast; Georgia—east-central Georgia

Food: aquatic insects, small crustaceans, plant matter

Reproduction: migrates upstream to spawn in late spring through early summer; males aggressively "head butt" to defend territory; males sometimes move stones around but do not build a significant nest; eggs are scattered over stones and left unattended

Average Size: 8 to 14 inches, 8 ounces

Records: none

Notes: The Creek Chubsucker is a thick, chubby sucker that prefers deep stream pools or clear lakes with good vegetative growth. The Creek Chubsucker's mouth is slightly upturned, indicating that they may feed higher in the water column than other suckers. Chubsuckers are very prolific and even a small number of breeding adults in a lake can produce large numbers of fry for game fish to feed on. Chubsuckers take a hook readily and are often caught by river fisherman drifting worms in deep pools.

Description: bright silver back and sides, often with a yellow tinge; fins clear; deep body with round, blunt head; leading edge of dorsal fin extends into a large, arching "quill"

Similar Species: Common Carp (pg. 76)

Quillback	Common Carp
mouth lacks barbels	barbels below mouth

QUILLBACK

Carpiodes cyprinus

Other Names: silver carp, carpsucker, lake quillback

Habitat: slow-flowing streams and rivers; backwaters and lakes, particularly areas with soft bottoms

Range: south-central Canada through the Great Lakes to the eastern US; south through the Mississippi drainage to the Gulf; Georgia—the Tennessee River drainage in northeast, scattered large impoundments

Food: insects, plant matter, decaying bottom material

Reproduction: spawns in late spring through early summer in tributaries or lake shallows; eggs are deposited in open areas over sand or a mud bottom

Average Size: 12 to 14 inches, 1 to 3 pounds

Records: state—none; North American—8 pounds, 13 ounces, Lake Winnebago, Wisconsin, 2003

Notes: In North America, there are four fish known as carpsuckers. The Quillback is the most common and widespread carpsucker and one of two found in Georgia. The River Carpsucker is the other. Quillbacks prefer medium to large rivers and large impoundments and even though they are not widespread in Georgia, they can be very common locally and very obvious during spawning runs. They are a schooling fish that filter feed along the bottom. Not often sought by anglers, they readily take wet flies and can be strong fighters when caught on light tackle. The flesh is white and very flavorful.

Description: dark gray back, silver sides; silver-white belly; lower fins white or reddish brown, red in breeding season; downturned sucker mouth; scales have a dark edge and no dark spot at point of attachment

Similar Species: Spotted Sucker (pg. 142)

Silver Redhorse

large protruding sucker mouth

Spotted Sucker

small sucker mouth

Silver Redhorse

dots on small scales forming lines

Spotted Sucker

large scales, no dots

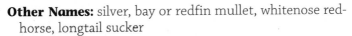
SILVER REDHORSE

Moxostoma anisurum

Other Names: silver, bay or redfin mullet, whitenose red-horse, longtail sucker

Habitat: clean streams and rivers with hard bottoms and deep pools; a few clear lakes

Range: Manitoba to the St. Lawrence drainage south to northern Alabama and Missouri; Georgia—east-central

Food: aquatic insects, small crustaceans and plant debris

Reproduction: spawns in early spring when the water reaches the high 50s; adults migrate into small tributary streams to lay eggs on shallow gravel bars in swift current near deepwater pools

Average Size: 11 to 22 inches, 2 to 5 pounds

Records: state—none; North American—11 pounds, 5 ounces, Brunet River, Wisconsin, 1983

Notes: There are ten fish in Georgia called redhorses. All are "sucker type fish" rather similar in appearance. They may look alike but each is a separate species and occupies its own biological niche. Each redhorse has a distinctive lip shape and can be easily told apart. Silver Redhorses inhabit the large to medium streams in east-central Georgia. They can be very abundant locally but normally are not common. They prefer deep pools and are readily caught with worms when fished near the bottom. All the redhorses require clean water with a hard substrate and are declining in numbers with increased siltation. Redhorses are bony but have firm, flavorful flesh. **139**

Description: back is dark olive-brown fading to yellow-brown; blotches on the sides; 4 to 5 irregular dark saddles; elongated body almost round in cross section; large head that is concave between the eyes; lower fins are dull red

Similar Species: Silver Redhorse (pg. 138), Spotted Sucker (pg. 142)

Northern Hog Sucker	**Silver Redhorse**	**Spotted Sucker**
head concave between eyes	head slightly humped between eyes	head flat between eyes

NORTHERN HOG SUCKER

Hypentelium nigricans

Other Names: hog molly, hammerhead, riffle or bigheaded sucker, crawl-a-bottom

Habitat: riffles and tailwaters of clear streams with hard bottoms; found in a few lakes near the mouths of tributary streams

Range: central and eastern Canada and the US south to Alabama and west to Oklahoma; Georgia—north and northeast

Food: small crustaceans, aquatic insects

Reproduction: spawns in April and May when water reaches the low 60s; males gather in riffles or downstream pools; females enter spawning areas just long enough to drop eggs, which are quickly fertilized by several males; no parental care

Average Size: 10 to 12 inches, 1 pound

Records: state—none; North American—1 pound, 12 ounces, Fox River, Wisconsin, 2004

Notes: Northern Hog Suckers are clean-water fish and well adapted to feed in moving water. They use their elongated shape and concave head to hold their place in riffles while turning over stones to release food. It is common for other fish to follow Hog Suckers to feed on what is stirred up. Hog Suckers are not of much interest to anglers but are sometimes caught by trout fishermen when working the edge of fast water.

141

Description: back dark green to olive-brown; sides coppery-green; scales have black squares that form lines; dorsal fin dark; the lower fins tinged orange; snout barely extends beyond upper lip

Similar Species: Northern Hog Sucker (pg. 140), Silver Redhorse (pg. 138)

Spotted Sucker
head flat between eyes

Northern Hog Sucker
head concave between eyes

Silver Redhorse
head slightly humped between eyes

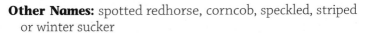

SPOTTED SUCKER

Catostomidae

Minytrema melanops

Other Names: spotted redhorse, corncob, speckled, striped or winter sucker

Habitat: slow-moving streams, rivers and backwaters

Range: Canada through the central and eastern US; from Texas and the Gulf States to the Carolinas; Georgia— statewide except north-central portion of the states

Food: insects, crustaceans, plant matter

Reproduction: spawns in early spring when water reaches the high 50s to low 60s; adults spawn in tributary riffles over gravel or coarse sand; females are attended by two males and deposit eggs with much splashing near the water surface

Average Size: 8 to 15 inches, 8 ounces to 1 pound

Records: state—none; North American—1 pound, 6 ounces, Catfish Creek, Texas, 2002

Notes: The Spotted Sucker is one of the most common fish in many Georgia rivers and one of the most important. Highly productive, it provides a large source of forage for game fish and is often used as a large bait minnow. Suckers are not the great consumers of fish eggs they were once thought to be, and the tremendous forage source young suckers pro- vide for game fish offsets any egg loss. Spotted Suckers are not often fished for but the flesh is firm with a fine flavor and is oily enough to make excellent smoked fish.

Description: dark green back; greenish sides often with dark lateral band; belly white to gray; large forward-facing mouth; lower jaw extends to rear margin of eye

Similar Species: Smallmouth Bass (pg. 150), Spotted Bass (pg. 152)

Largemouth Bass	Smallmouth Bass	Spotted Bass
mouth extends well beyond brown eye	mouth does not extend beyond red eye	mouth does not extend beyond orange eye

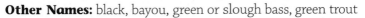

LARGEMOUTH BASS

Centrarchidae

Micropterus salmoides

Other Names: black, bayou, green or slough bass, green trout

Habitat: shallow, fertile, weedy lakes and river backwaters; weedy bays and extensive weedbeds of large lakes

Range: southern Canada through the United States into Mexico, extensively introduced worldwide; Georgia— common throughout state

Food: small fish, frogs, insects, crayfish

Reproduction: spawns when water temperature reaches 60 degrees; male builds nest in small clearings in weedbeds 2 to 8 feet deep; male guards nest and fry until the "brood swarm" disperses

Average Size: 12 to 20 inches, 1 to 5 pounds

Records: state—22 pounds, 4 ounces, Montgomery Lake, Georgia, 1932; North American—22 pounds, 4 ounces, Montgomery Lake, Georgia, 1932

Notes: The Largemouth Bass is the most sought-after game fish in North America. This denizen of the weedbeds is a voracious carnivore and will eat anything that fits into its mouth. Largemouths are common in lakes and wide streams with weedbeds less than 20 feet deep. Largemouths are often 1 to 3 pounds, but 8 and 9 pound fish are not uncommon. They are fine table fare when under 2 pounds and taken from clear water, but are not known for table quality when large or taken from muddy water.

145

Description: dark green to black with greenish-brown sides and dark bars; red eye; dark stripes extending from eye; lower jaw extends to front of eye; shallow notch between hard and soft dorsal fins; scales on base of dorsal and anal fins; 16 to 17 scale rows below the lateral line and 67 to 72 scales in the lateral line

Similar Species: Largemouth Bass (pg. 144), Shoal Bass (pg. 148)

Redeye/Shoal Bass	Largemouth Bass	Redeye Bass	Shoal Bass
mouth does not extend past eye	mouth extends well beyond eye	white edge on top and bottom of caudal fin	no white on caudal fin

REDEYE BASS
Micropterus coosae

Other Names: Flint River, Chipola or Coosa bass

Habitat: rocky shallows in rivers and small streams

Range: Alabama, Georgia and South Carolina; Georgia—southeast corner of the state

Food: small fish, frogs, insects and crayfish

Reproduction: ascends small tributary streams to spawn when water temperatures reach 60 degrees; males build nest, then guard the nest and fry; does not reproduce well in waters without a current

Average Size: 10 to 18 inches, 2 to 4 pounds

Records: no state records for Redeye or Shoal Bass are kept due to the difficulty in differentiating between them

Notes: The Redeye Bass is primarily a stream fish though it has been successfully introduced in a few lakes. In Georgia, Redeye Bass are most abundant in streams that drain into the Florida Panhandle. Redeyes prefer the cover of brush piles or undercut banks at the edge of faster water. The Redeye Bass is closely related to the Shoal Bass and often there is a great deal of confusion in separating the two and the records reflect this confusion. The Redeye is a very sporting small fish for light-tackle fisherman and has an ardent following among some fly fishermen.

Description: dark green back; greenish sides with dark blotches; dark spot on gill and base of tail; red eye; dark stripes extend from eye; lower jaw extends to front of eye; shallow notch between dorsal fins with scales at their base; no red on caudal fin; 18 to 19 scale rows below the lateral line and 72 to 77 scales in the lateral line

Similar Species: Largemouth Bass (pg. 144), Redeye Bass (pg. 146)

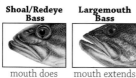

Shoal/Redeye Bass

mouth does not extend past eye

Largemouth Bass

mouth extends well beyond eye

Shoal Bass

no white on caudal fin

Redeye Bass

white edge on top and bottom of caudal fin

SHOAL BASS

Micropterus cataractae

Centrarchidae

Other Names: Flint River or Chipola bass

Habitat: rocky shallows in rivers and small streams

Range: Florida Panhandle and southern Georgia; Georgia—rivers at the Florida Panhandle border

Food: small fish, frogs, insects and crayfish

Reproduction: ascends small tributary streams to spawn when water temperatures reach 60 degrees; males build nest then guard the nest and fry

Average Size: 10 to 18 inches, 2 to 4 pounds

Records: state—no records for Redeye or Shoal Bass are kept due to the difficulty in differentiating between them; North American—8 pounds, 12 ounces, Apalachicola River, Florida, 1995 (IFGA)

Notes: For a long time, Shoal Bass were considered to be a subspecies of the Redeye Bass and there is still a great deal of confusion concerning the two and the records reflect this confusion. In the late '90s, Shoal Bass were designated as a separate species. It is now thought that the Shoal Bass is the predominant fast-water river bass in some streams near the Florida line. The surest way to differentiate between the two species is by counting scales. Shoal Bass have 18 to 19 scale rows below the lateral line and 72 to 77 scales in the lateral line. Redeye Bass have 16 to 17 scale rows below the lateral line and 67 to 72 scales in the lateral line.

149

Description: back and sides mottled dark green to bronze or pale gold, often with dark vertical bands; white belly; stout body; large, forward-facing mouth; red eye

Similar Species: Largemouth Bass (pg. 144), Spotted Bass (pg. 152)

Smallmouth Bass	**Largemouth Bass**	**Spotted Bass**
mouth does not extend beyond red eye	mouth extends well beyond brown eye	mouth does not extend beyond orange eye

Smallmouth Bass	**Spotted Bass**	**Smallmouth Bass**	**Spotted Bass**
bronze bars on sides	lines of dots on lower sides	scales on base of tail/anal fins, no spot at base of tail	no scales on base of tail/anal fins, spot at base of tail

SMALLMOUTH BASS

Micropterus dolomieu

Other Names: bronzeback, brown or redeye bass, redeye

Habitat: clear, swift-flowing streams and rivers; clear lakes with gravel or rocky shorelines

Range: extensively introduced throughout North America, Europe and Asia; Georgia—large northern impoundments and a few rivers

Food: insects, small fish, crayfish

Reproduction: male builds a nest in 3 to 10 feet of water over open gravel beds when water temperatures reach the mid-to-high 60s; nest is often near logs or boulders; male aggressively guards the nest and young until fry disperse

Average Size: 12 to 20 inches, 1 to 4 pounds

Records: state—7 pounds, 2 ounces, Lake Chatuge, 1973; North American—11 pounds, 15 ounces, Dale Hollow Lake, Tennessee, 1955

Notes: Smallmouth Bass are a world-class game fish noted for strong fights and acrobatic jumps. Native to the Tennessee River drainage in Georgia, they have been extensively introduced in northern Georgia and around the world. Though the range of this slow-maturing fish has expanded, its numbers are decreasing due to overfishing and habitat loss. Smallmouth Bass prefer deeper water than the weedbeds preferred by its larger cousin, the Largemouth Bass. Their flesh is firm, succulent and regarded by some anglers as second only to Walleye as table fare.

Description: dark green back with light green sides; side blotches form a dark stripe, with dark spots above; light spots on each scale forming lines on lower sides; dark lines extend from orange eye

Similar Species: Largemouth Bass (pg. 144), Smallmouth Bass (pg. 150)

Spotted Bass

mouth does not extend beyond orange eye

Smallmouth Bass

mouth does not extend beyond red eye

Largemouth Bass

mouth extends well beyond brown eye

Spotted Bass

lines of dots on lower sides

Smallmouth Bass

bronze bars on sides

Spotted Bass

no scales on base of tail/anal fins

Smallmouth Bass

scales on base of tail/anal fins

SPOTTED BASS

Micropterus punctulatus

Other Names: Kentucky, speckled or yellow bass, spottys

Habitat: deep, silted pools in sluggish, medium-to-large streams; larger lakes and reservoirs

Range: the Ohio and Mississippi drainage in the southern US from Florida to Texas; Georgia—native to the northeast portion of the state, introduced widely

Food: small fish and crayfish

Reproduction: when water temperatures reach the mid- to high 60s in May and June, males build a nest in open gravel beds 3 to 4 feet deep; male aggressively guards the nest and young

Average Size: 8 to 18 inches, eight ounces to 3 pounds

Records: state—8 pounds, 2 ounces, Lake Burton, 2005; North American—10 pounds, 4 ounces, Pine Flat Lake, California, 2001

Notes: The Spotted Bass is native to northeast Georgia but has been introduced widely and is now very abundant in some impoundments. In terms of habit, Spotted Bass share traits with both Largemouth and Smallmouth Bass. Spotted Bass are found in slower, deep pools, whereas Smallmouths prefer stream riffles and Largemouths inhabit the edges of weedbeds. In reservoirs, Spotted Bass seek deeper water than Smallmouth Bass. Spotted Bass can tolerate higher turbidity than other bass. In Georgia, Spotted Bass are smaller than Largemouths but are larger than Smallmouths.

153

Description: dark green back; greenish brown sides with dark blotches; lower sides and pectoral fins are turquoise; red eye; lower jaw extends to eye; shallow notch between hard and soft dorsal fins; scales on base of dorsal or anal fin

Similar Species: Largemouth Bass (pg. 144), Shoal Bass (pg. 148), Redeye Bass (pg. 146)

Suwannee Bass

mouth extends to center of eye

Largemouth Bass

mouth extends beyond eye

Suwannee Bass

chin, breast and belly turquoise

Largemouth Bass

chin, breast and belly dirty white

Suwannee Bass

gray-green tail

Redeye/Shoal Bass

red tail

SUWANNEE BASS

Centrarchidae

Micropterus notius

Other Names: blue belly, river or riffle bass

Habitat: rocky riffles of medium to large rivers

Range: restricted to northern Florida and southern Georgia; Georgia—a few streams in the Suwannee River drainage

Food: small fish, frogs, insects and crayfish

Reproduction: spawns when water temperatures reach 60 degrees; males build nest in the quiet, weedy water along stream edges; males guard the nest and fry

Average Size: 8 to 10 inches, 1 to 2 pounds

Records: state—3 pounds, 9 ounces, Ochlocknee River, Georgia, 1984; North American—3 pounds, 9 ounces, Ochlocknee River, Georgia, 1984

Notes: Suwannee Bass are a small bass that rarely exceed 12 inches. They are closely related to Redeye and Spotted Bass. Suwannee Bass are river fish and do not naturally occur in lakes. Native to the Suwannee river drainage, they have been introduced into the Aucilla-Wacissa river system in recent years. Though small, they are hard fighters in fast water and prized by fly-fishermen who fish for them in small tributaries of the Suwannee River.

Description: black to olive back; silver sides with dark green to black blotches; back with a more pronounced arch and depression above eye than White Crappie

Similar Species: White Crappie (pg. 158)

Black Crappie
usually 7 to 8 spines in dorsal fin

White Crappie
usually 5 to 6 spines in dorsal fin

Black Crappie
dorsal fin length equal to distance from eye to dorsal

White Crappie
dorsal fin shorter than distance from eye to dorsal

BLACK CRAPPIE
Pomoxis nigromaculatus

Other Names: speckled perch, speck, papermouth

Habitat: quiet, clear water of streams and midsized lakes; often associated with vegetation but may roam over deep, open basins and flats, particularly during winter

Range: southern Manitoba through the Atlantic and south-eastern states, introduced in the West; Georgia—statewide

Food: small fish, aquatic insects, zooplankton

Reproduction: spawns in shallow weedbeds from May to June when water temperatures reach the high 50s; male builds circular nest in fine gravel or sand and then guards the eggs and young until fry begin feeding

Average Size: 7 to 12 inches, eight ounces to 1 pound

Records: state—4 pounds, 4 ounces, Acrees Lake, 1971; North American—6 pounds, Westwego Canal, Louisiana, 1969

Notes: The Black Crappie is the most widespread Crappie species in North America and native to the Atlantic seaboard. They are found in most lakes and slow moving streams in Georgia that have clear water and good vegetative growth. Black Crappies are a schooling fish and when not spawning are often found suspended in deeper water. They nest in colonies and frequently gather in large feeding schools in winter. Black Crappies are sought for their sweet-tasting, white fillets, but not for their fighting ability.

157

Description: greenish back; silvery green to white sides with 7 to 9 dark vertical bars; the only sunfish with six spines in both the dorsal and anal fins

Similar Species: Black Crappie (pg. 156)

White Crappie	**Black Crappie**	**White Crappie**	**Black Crappie**
usually 5 to 6 spines in dorsal fin	usually 7 to 8 spines in dorsal fin	dorsal fin shorter than distance from eye to dorsal	dorsal fin length equal to distance from eye to dorsal

WHITE CRAPPIE

Pomoxis annularis

Other Names: silver, pale or ringed crappie, papermouth

Habitat: slightly silty streams and midsized lakes; prefers less vegetation than Black Crappie

Range: North Dakota south and east to the Gulf and Atlantic states except peninsular Florida; Georgia—scattered throughout state

Food: aquatic insects, zooplankton, small fish

Reproduction: spawns on a firm sand or gravel bottom when water temperatures approach 60 degrees; male builds shallow, round nest; male guards eggs and young after spawning

Average Size: 8 to 10 inches, 5 to 16 ounces

Records: state—5 pounds, Bibb County Pond, 1984; North American—5 pounds, 3 ounces, Enid Dam, Mississippi, 1957

Notes: Native to the Mississippi and Tennessee River drainages, White Crappies have now been widely introduced in Georgia but still are not as common as Black Crappies. They prefer deeper, less vegetated water than Black Crappies and can tolerate more turbidity. Due to its tolerance of turbid water, there is some indication of a positive relation between the Common Carp and the White Crappie. Lakes that have large populations of carp tend to have more White Crappies than Black Crappies. Both crappies are more active in cold water than other sunfish and are popular sunfish all the year.

159

Description: dark olive to green on back, blending to silver-gray, copper, orange, purple or brown on sides; 5 to 9 dark vertical bars on sides that fade with age; yellow belly and copper breast; large, dark gill spot with light margin; dark spot on dorsal fin

Similar Species: Green Sunfish (pg. 164), Redbreast Sunfish (pg. 166)

Bluegill	**Green Sunfish**	**Bluegill**	**Redbreast Sunfish**
small mouth	large mouth	long, pointed pectoral fin	short, round pectoral fin

BLUEGILL

Centrarchidae

Lepomis macrochirus

Other Names: bream, sun perch, blue sunfish, copperbelly, strawberry bass

Habitat: medium to large streams and most lakes with weedy bays or shorelines

Range: southern Canada through the southern states into Mexico; Georgia—common throughout state

Food: aquatic insects, snails, small fish

Reproduction: spawns from when water temperature reaches the high 60s to low 80s; male builds a nest in vegetation in a colony of other nests; male guards nest and fry

Average Size: 6 to 9 inches, 5 to 8 ounces

Records: state—3 pounds, 5 ounces, Shamrock Lake, 1977; North American—4 pounds, 12 ounces, Ketona Lake, Alabama, 1950

Notes: Bluegills are native to Georgia and are the most popular panfish here and throughout the United States. They have small mouths and feed mostly on aquatic insects and small fish. Bluegills prefer deep weedbeds at the edge of open water. Bluegills move to the surface to feed more frequently than other panfish, making them popular with fly fishermen. Many lakes have large populations of hybrid sunfish, crosses between Bluegills and Green Sunfish. Painted Bream are not a separate species, but a variety of bluegills with a pink throat and dark blotches on the sides.

Description: olive-green to silver-green back and sides; longitudinal stripes of brown spots on sides; dark wedge-shaped bar under eye; latterly compressed body; anal and dorsal fins nearly equal length; dark spot on dorsal fin of young fish; small mouth

Similar Species: Green Sunfish (pg. 164), Redbreast Sunfish (pg. 166)

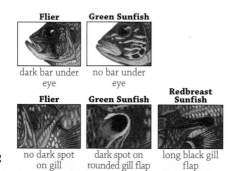

Flier	Green Sunfish
dark bar under eye	no bar under eye

Flier	Green Sunfish	Redbreast Sunfish
no dark spot on gill	dark spot on rounded gill flap	long black gill flap

FLIER

Centrarchus macropterus

Other Names: spotfin, silver, round or swamp sunfish

Habitat: weedy, quiet waters with a soft bottom in lakes, creeks, coastal swamps

Range: coastal states from Virginia to eastern Texas, Mississippi Valley through the Ohio Valley; Georgia—southern lowlands

Food: aquatic insects, zooplankton, small fish

Reproduction: nests in late spring or early summer in dense vegetation; nests are solitary or in small groups, males guard nest and young

Average Size: 4 to 6 inches, 4 ounces

Records: state—1 pound, 4 ounces, Lowndes County Pond, 1996 (not recorded as a North American record); North American—1 pound, 2 ounces, Pope's Pond, Georgia, 1995

Notes: Fliers are small sunfish native to the southern Atlantic coast. This sunfish can withstand lower oxygen levels and higher acidity than most other sunfish. It is very common in still, swampy water. Rarely over 6 inches long, Fliers are too small to be an important panfish but they readily bite and can be proficient bait robbers. When large enough to eat, Fliers have flaky, white flesh and fine flavor. Though not a prized panfish, fliers are good predators of mosquito larvae, and small ones should be carefully returned to the water.

163

Description: dark green back with dark olive to bluish sides; yellow to cream belly; scales flecked with yellow, producing a brassy appearance; dark gill spot with a light margin; large mouth and thick lips

Similar Species: Bluegill (pg. 160), Redear Sunfish (pg. 168)

Green Sunfish	Bluegill	Redear Sunfish
prominent light margin around dark gill spot	dark gill spot with no clear margin	red-orange margin around dark gill spot

GREEN SUNFISH

Lepomis cyanellus

Other Names: green perch, sand bass

Habitat: warm, weedy, shallow lakes and the backwaters of slow-moving streams

Range: most of the United States into Mexico, excluding Florida and the Rocky Mountains; Georgia—statewide

Food: aquatic insects, small crustaceans and fish

Reproduction: male builds nest in less than a foot of weedy water when temperatures are 60 to 80 degrees; may produce two broods per year; male guards nest and fans eggs until hatching

Average Size: 4 to 6 inches, less than 8 ounces

Records: state—1 pound, 7 ounces, private pond, 2006; North American—2 pounds, 2 ounces, Stockton Lake, Missouri, 1971

Notes: Green Sunfish are often mistaken for Bluegills but are not as deep-bodied and have a much bigger mouth. Green Sunfish prefer shallower weedbeds than Bluegills and are very tolerant of turbid water and low oxygen levels. They thrive in warm, weedy lakes and backwaters. Green Sunfish stunt easily, filling some lakes with three-inch-long "potato chips." Green Sunfish sometimes hybridize with other sunfish species, producing large, aggressive offspring, but in the end these crosses result in poor panfish populations overall.

Description: dark olive-green back; olive sides; yellow-orange belly; bright yellow-orange breast; gill flap long, black and narrower than the eye; tail slightly forked

Similar Species: Bluegill (pg. 160), Green Sunfish (pg. 164)

Redbreast Sunfish	**Bluegill**	**Redbreast Sunfish**	**Green Sunfish**
short, round pectoral fin	long, pointed pectoral fin	long, narrow, dark gill flap	short gill flap with round dark spot

REDBREAST SUNFISH

Centrarchidae

Lepomis auritus

Other Names: yellowbelly or longear sunfish, sun perch, redbreast bream

Habitat: rocky riffles in streams with medium current; occasionally lakes or reservoirs

Range: Atlantic drainage from southern New York to Florida; Georgia—statewide except the northeast corner of the state

Food: aquatic insects, crustaceans, small fish

Reproduction: spawns in May and June when water temperature reaches the high 60s; male builds a small, round nest in weedbeds away from the current; male defends nest

Average Size: 4 to 8 inches, 4 ounces

Records: state—1 pound, 11 ounces, Coweta County Pond, 1986; North American—2 pounds, 1 ounce, Suwannee River, Florida, 1988

Notes: The Redbreast Sunfish is a small sunfish native to the Atlantic drainage east of the Alleghenies and has been introduced throughout the Southeast. It prefers streams, but is frequently found in reservoirs and impoundments. Redbreast Sunfish are often found around rocks, logs or undercut banks near moving water. They are slightly more nocturnal than other sunfish. A popular panfish in many areas, they bite aggressively on small artificial lures and live bait both day and night.

Description: back and sides bronze to dark green, fading to light green; sides have faint vertical bars and small spots; long, pointed pectoral fins; gill flap short with dark spot and red margin in males; breast yellow or orange

Similar Species: Bluegill (pg. 160), Redbreast Sunfish (pg. 166)

Redear Sunfish	**Bluegill**	**Redbreast Sunfish**
red-orange margin on gill spot	round gill spot with clear margin	long, narrow, dark gill flap

REDEAR SUNFISH

Centrarchidae

Lepomis microlophus

Other Names: shellcracker, stumpknocker, yellow bream

Habitat: congregates around stumps and logs in low to moderate vegetation in lakes and swamps and large, quiet streams; prefers sand or gravel bottoms, frequents brackish water

Range: the northern Midwest through the South, introduced in the West; Georgia—common statewide except in far north

Food: mainly mollusks

Reproduction: males build and guard nest in shallow vegetated water in spring when water temperatures reach high 60s; may produce second brood well into summer

Average Size: 8 to 10 inches, 8 ounces to 1 pound

Records: state—4 pounds, 6 ounces, Richmond County Pond, 1986; North American—5 pounds, 7 1/2 ounces, Diversion Canal, South Carolina, 1998

Notes: The Redear is a large, highly regarded Southern sunfish that has now been introduced in many northern states. Redears are native to Georgia and are the state's largest most common and popular sunfish. The Redear is often found in dense vegetation where it feeds on snails attached to plant stems. This makes it somewhat harder to locate and catch than other sunfish. The Redear is more tolerant of brackish waters than most sunfish and is often found along the deepwater edges of salt marshes and coastal stream mouths.

Description: brown to olive-green back and sides with an overall bronze appearance; each scale on sides has a dark spot; red eye; thicker, heavier body than other sunfish; large mouth

Similar Species: Green Sunfish (pg. 164), Warmouth (pg. 174), Black Bass (pp. 144-154)

Rock Bass

dark squares on each scale

Black Bass

no dark squares on scales

Rock Bass

6 spines in anal fin

Green Sunfish

3 spines in anal fin

Warmouth

3 spines on anal fin

ROCK BASS

Ambloplites rupestris

Other Names: redeye, goggle eye, rock sunfish

Habitat: clear lakes and midsized streams with vegetation and firm or rocky bottoms

Range: southern Canada through the central and eastern United States to the northern edge of the Gulf States; Georgia—native to northern highlands and introduced further south

Food: crayfish, aquatic insects, small fish

Reproduction: spawns when water temperature reaches the high 60s to 70s; male builds a nest in coarse gravel in submerged vegetation less than 3 feet deep; male guards eggs and fry

Average Size: 8 to 10 inches, 8 ounces to 1 pound

Records: state—none; North American—3 pounds, York River, Ontario, 1974

Notes: A common sunfish in clear lakes and streams of northern Georgia, the Rock Bass can be very plentiful in some waters. Nevertheless, few anglers target them, as its flesh is somewhat more strongly flavored than that of Bluegills and Redears. In both lakes and streams, Rock Bass are normally found over a rocky or gravel substrate, even when vegetation is present. Rock Bass are frequently found in schools that stay put, not moving from their home territories. Once these schools are located, Rock Bass are easy to catch.

Description: olive-green to black back; scales on the sides each have a dark brown spot at base producing regular rows of spots; lower sides and belly dull red to reddish-brown; plain dark gill spot with light margin

Similar Species: Bluegill (pg. 160), Redear Sunfish (pg. 168)

Spotted Sunfish	Bluegill	Spotted Sunfish	Redear Sunfish
no blotch near rear base of dorsal fin	blotch near rear base of dorsal fin	rounded pectoral fin	pointed pectoral fin

SPOTTED SUNFISH

Lepomis punctatus

Other Names: stumpknocker, spotted bream, bream

Habitat: slow-moving, weedy streams and rivers with hard bottoms

Range: South Carolina south to Florida, west to Texas, north up the Mississippi River basin to Illinois; Georgia— common statewide except northeast corner

Food: aquatic insects and small fish

Reproduction: males build and guard a solitary nest in shallow, well-vegetated water in spring when water temperatures reach the high 60s; males guard nest very aggressively

Average Size: 4 to 6 inches, 4 ounces

Records: State—10 ounces, Brier Creek, 2003; North American—2 pounds, 11 ounces, Hall's Lake, Georgia, 1985 (IGFA, not recorded with the state)

Notes: The Spotted Sunfish is most often found in weedy, slow-moving streams. In many such streams it is the predominant sunfish. Spotted Sunfish have a tendency to feed on, or near, the bottom more than other sunfish. However, Spotted Sunfish are aggressive feeders, and though often too small to keep, they can be locally very abundant and a persistent bait robber in some streams.

Description: back and sides greenish-gray to brown with faint
  vertical bands; stout body; large mouth; red eyes; 3 to 5
  streaks radiate from eyes; dark spots on dorsal and anal fins

Similar Species: Bluegill (pg. 160), Green Sunfish (pg. 164),
  Redear Sunfish (pg. 168), Rock Bass (pg. 170)

Warmouth	**Bluegill**	**Green Sunfish**
jaw extends to middle of eye	small mouth does not extend to eye	jaw does not extend to middle of eye

Warmouth	**Redear Sunfish**	**Rock Bass**
light margin on gill spot	orange-red margin on gill spot	dark gill spot lacks light margin

WARMOUTH

Lepomis gulosus

Centararchadie

Other Names: goggle eye, widemouth sunfish, stumpknocker, weed bass

Habitat: heavy weeds in turbid lakes, swamps and slow-moving streams

Range: the southern US from Texas to Florida and north to the southern Great Lakes region; Georgia—statewide

Food: prefers crayfish, eats aquatic insects and small fish

Reproduction: when water temperatures reach the high 60s to 70s, males build nest in coarse gravel in submerged vegetation less than 3 feet deep; males guard eggs and fry

Average Size: 11 inches, 8 to 12 ounces

Records: state—2 pounds, private pond, 1974; North American—2 pounds, 7 ounces, Yellow River, Florida, 1985

Notes: This secretive sunfish is common in the shallow lakes and swamps of southern Georgia and uncommon to rare in the rest of the state. Warmouths are solitary, aggressive sight-feeders that are often found around rocks and submerged stumps when not hiding in dense vegetation. They prefer cloudy water with a soft bottom and can withstand low oxygen levels, high silt loads and temperatures into the 90s. The Warmouths in many areas are small and off the radar screen of most fishermen, but when large, it is a scrappy, strong fighter that rivals even Smallmouth Bass when caught on light tackle.

Description: gray-black back; silver sides with 6 to 8 uninterrupted black stripes; front of dorsal fin separated from soft-rayed rear portion; lower jaw protrudes beyond snout

Similar Species: Striped Bass Hybrid (pg. 178), White Perch (pg. 182), Striped Bass (pg. 180)

White Bass	Striped Bass	White Bass	White Perch
single spine on gill cover	two spines on gill cover	horizontal black stripes	no stripes except on lateral line

White Bass	Striped Bass	Striped Bass Hybrid
single tooth patch on tongue	two tooth patches on tongue	two tooth patches on tongue

WHITE BASS

Morone chrysops

Other Names: lake, sand or silver bass, streaker

Habitat: rivers, large lakes and impoundments with relatively clear water

Range: the Great Lakes region to the Eastern Seaboard, through the southeast to the Gulf and west to Texas; Georgia—native to the Tennessee drainage, introduced to other large impoundments

Food: small fish

Reproduction: spawns in late spring or early summer; eggs spread in open water over gravel beds or rubble 6 to 10 feet deep; some populations migrate to narrow bays or up tributary streams to spawn

Average Size: 9 to 18 inches, 8 ounces to 2 pounds

Records: state—5 pounds, 1 ounce, Lake Lanier, 1971; North American—6 pounds, 13 ounces, Lake Orange, Virginia, 1989

Notes: The White Bass is native to the Great Lakes and Mississippi basins and the lower Tennessee drainage but probably did not reach much of Georgia until recent introductions. It quickly became established and has since become one of the popular sport fish of large impoundments. The flesh is somewhat soft but has a good flavor that can be improved if the fish is put on ice and chilled as soon as it is caught.

Description: dark gray back; bright silver sides with 7 or 8 indistinct stripes; dorsal fin separated, front part has hard spines, rear part has soft rays; two tooth patches, one on back of the tongue

Similar Species: Striped Bass (pg. 180), White Bass (pg. 176)

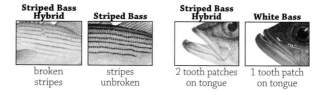

Striped Bass Hybrid	Striped Bass	Striped Bass Hybrid	White Bass
broken stripes	stripes unbroken	2 tooth patches on tongue	1 tooth patch on tongue

Moronidae

STRIPED BASS HYBRID

Morone saxatilis x Morone chrysops

Other Names: white striper, whiterock, wiper

Habitat: open water of large lakes and slow-moving rivers

Range: stocked in about 40 US states; Georgia—stocked in a few large impoundments

Food: small fish, insects, crustaceans

Reproduction: hatchery-produced hybrid that is only occasionally fertile

Average Size: 1 to 2 feet, 5 to 10 pounds

Records: state—25 pounds, 8 ounces, Lake Chatuge, 1995; North American—27 pounds, 5 ounces, Greer's Ferry Lake, Arkansas, 1997

Notes: There are two Striped Bass Hybrids. The Sunshine Bass is a hatchery cross between a male Striped Bass and a female White Bass. The Palmetto Bass is the opposite; it is a cross between a male White Bass and a female Striped Bass. Both hybrids are fertile but there is only limited reproduction. Many states now raise large numbers of these hybrids to stock in waters too warm to support Striped Bass. This hard-fighting, tasty hybrid bass has now become a favorite with anglers where there are not good Striper populations. The Hybrid Striped Bass is also becoming an important aquaculture fish, supplying filets for the grocery store and restaurant market.

Description: dark gray back; bright silver sides with 7 or 8 distinct stripes; jaw protrudes beyond snout; dorsal fin separated, front part hard spines, rear part soft rays

Similar Species: White Bass (pg. 176), Striped Bass Hybrid (pg. 178)

Striped Bass	**Striped Bass Hybrid**	**Striped Bass**	**White Bass**
unbroken horizontal stripes	broken horizontal stripes	two tooth patches on tongue	single tooth patch on tongue

STRIPED BASS

Morone saxatilis

Other Names: striper, streaker, surf bass, rockfish

Habitat: coastal areas and associated spawning streams; land-locked in some large lakes and reservoirs

Range: the Atlantic coast from Maine to northern Florida and the Gulf Coast; Georgia—coastline and coastal streams, a few large inland impoundments

Food: small fish

Reproduction: spawns in freshwater streams; eggs deposited in riffles at the mouth of large tributaries; eggs must remain suspended to hatch

Average Size: 18 to 30 inches, 10 to 20 pounds

Records: state—63 pounds, Oconee River, 1967; North American—78 pounds, 8 ounces, Atlantic City, New Jersey, 1992

Notes: Striped Bass are a coastal marine fish native to Georgia. Striped Bass are anadromous, living in salt water and migrating into fresh water to spawn. When the Santee-Cooper Dam was built, it trapped some Striped Bass; these adapted to a freshwater existence and now spawn in tributary streams. Throughout the US there are many introduced inland populations that are maintained with hatchery produced fish, including some in Georgia. The introduction of the Striped Bass has created an exciting sport fishery in many large reservoirs. While the marine population of Striped Bass is declining, the "man-made" populations are thriving.

181

Description: olive to blackish-green back; silver-green sides with no stripes; front spiny dorsal fin connected by a small membrane to the soft ray back portion

Similar Species: White Bass (pg. 176)

White Perch

no stripes except on lateral line

White Bass

horizontal black stripes

WHITE PERCH

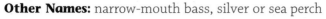

Moronidae

Morone americana

Other Names: narrow-mouth bass, silver or sea perch

Habitat: brackish water in coastal areas; near-shore areas of the Great Lakes; expanding range into smaller freshwater lakes and streams

Range: the Mississippi River drainage south to the Gulf of Mexico, Atlantic coast from Maine to South Carolina; Georgia—few streams and lakes

Reproduction: spawns in late spring over gravel bars of tributary streams

Average Size: 6 to 8 inches, 1 pound or less

Records: state—none; North American—4 pounds, 12 ounces, Messalonskee Lake, Maine, 1949

Notes: The White Perch is a coastal Atlantic species that inhabits brackish water inlets and streams. White Perch are not native as far south as Georgia but are quickly expanding their range, often into many freshwater habitats in the South and Midwest. These new introductions often occur in places where they are unwanted. A small, schooling panfish, the White Perch migrates up coastal streams to spawn and is very popular with many salt marsh anglers in the east, and is now becoming popular with some freshwater fisherman. The flesh is firm and white with a good flavor.

183

GLOSSARY

adipose fin a small, fleshy fin without rays, located on the midline of the fish's back between the dorsal fin and the tail

air bladder a balloon-like organ located in the gut area of a fish, used to control buoyancy—and in the respiration of some species such as gar; also called "swim bladder" or "gas bladder"

anadromous a fish that hatches in fresh water, migrates to the ocean, then re-enters streams or rivers from the sea (or large inland body of water) to spawn

anal fin a single fin located on the underside near the tail

anterior toward the front of a fish, opposite of posterior

bands horizontal markings running lengthwise along the side of a fish

barbel thread-like sensory structures on a fish's head often near the mouth, commonly called "whiskers"; used for taste or smell

bars vertical markings on the side of a fish

brood swarm a large group or "cloud" of young fish such as Black Bullheads

carnivore a species that subsists on animal flesh

catadromous a fish that lives in fresh water and migrates into salt water to spawn, such as the American Eel

caudal fin the tail or tail fin

caudal peduncle the portion of the fish's body located between the anal fin and the beginning of the tail

crustacean a crayfish, water flea, crab or other animal belonging to group of mostly aquatic species that have paired antennae, jointed legs and an exterior skeleton (exoskeleton); common food for many fish

dorsal relating to the top of the fish, on or near the back; opposite of the ventral, or lower, part of the fish

dorsal fin the fin or fins located along the top of a fish's back

exotic a foreign species not native to a watershed

fingerling a juvenile fish, generally 1 to 10 inches in length, in its first year of life

fork length the overall length of fish from the mouth to the deepest part of the tail notch

fry recently hatched young fish that have already absorbed their yolk sacs

game fish a species regulated by laws for recreational fishing

gills organs used in aquatic respiration (breathing)

gill cover large bone covering the fish's gills, also called opercle or operculum

gill flap also called ear flap; fleshy projection on the back edge of the gill cover of some fish such as Bluegill

gill raker a comb-like projection from the gill arch

ichthyologist a scientist who studies fish

invertebrates animals without backbones, such as insects, leeches and earthworms

kype hooked jaw acquired by some trout and salmon mainly during breeding season

lateral line a series of pored scales along the side of a fish that contain organs used to detect vibrations

mandible lower jaw

mollusk an invertebrate with a smooth, soft body such as a clam or a snail, often having an outer shell

native an indigenous or naturally occurring species

omnivore a fish or animal that eats plants and animal matter

otolith calcium concentration found in the inner ear of fish; used to determine age of some fish; also called ear bone

opercle the bone covering the gills, also called the gill cover or operculum

panfish small freshwater game fish that can be fried whole in a pan, such as Black Crappie, Bluegill and Yellow Perch

pectoral fins paired fins on the side of the fish located just behind the gills

pelvic fins paired fins located below or behind the pectoral fins on the bottom (ventral portion) of the fish

plankton floating or weakly swimming aquatic plants and animals, including larval fish, that drift with the current; often eaten by fish; individual organisms are called plankters

posterior toward the back of a fish, opposite of anterior

range the geographic region in which a species is found

ray, hard stiff fin support; resembles a spine but is jointed

ray, soft flexible fin support, sometimes branched

redd a nest-like depression made by a male or female fish during spawning, often refers to nest of trout and salmon species

roe fish eggs

scales small, flat plates covering the outer skin of many fish

spawning the process of fish reproduction; involves females laying eggs and males fertilizing them to produce young fish

spine stiff, non-jointed structures found along with soft rays in some fins

spiracle an opening on the posterior portion of the head above and behind the eye

standard length length of the fish from the mouth to the end of the vertebral column

substrate bottom composition of a lake, stream or river

subtenninal mouth a mouth below the snout of the fish

swim bladder see air bladder

terminal mouth forward-facing

total length length of fish from the mouth to the tail compressed to its fullest length

tributary a stream that feeds into another stream, river or lake

turbid cloudy; water clouded by suspended sediments or plant matter that limits visibility and the passage of light

vent the opening at the end of the digestive tract

ventral the underside of the fish

vertebrate an animal with a backbone

zooplankton the animal component of plankton; tiny animals that float or swim weakly; common food for small fish

INDEX

PRIMARY REFERENCES

Etnier, D. A. and Starnes, W. C. 1993
The Fishes of Tennessee
University of Tennessee Press

Jenkins, R. E. and Burkhead, N. M. 1994
Freshwater Fishes of Virginia
American Fisheries Society

Laerm, J. and Freeman, B. J. 1986
Fishes of the Okefenokee Swamp
The University of Georgia Press

Lee, D. S. et al. 1980
Atlas of North American Freshwater Fishes
North Carolina State Museum of Natural History

McClane, A. J. 1978
Freshwater Fishes of North America
Henry Holt and Company

Menhinick, E. F. 1991
The Freshwater Fishes of North Carolina
North Carolina Wildlife Resources Commission

Page, L. M. and Burr, B. M. 1991
Freshwater Fishes, Peterson Field Guide
Houghton Mifflin Company

Rohde, F. C., Arndt, R. G., Lindquist, D. G., & Parnell, J. F. 1994
Freshwater Fishes of the Carolinas, Virginia, Maryland, & Delaware
The University of North Carolina Press

ABOUT THE AUTHOR

Dave Bosanko was born in Kansas and studied engineering before following his love of nature to degrees in biology and chemistry from Emporia State University. He spent thirty years as staff biologist at two of the University of Minnesota's field stations. Though his training was in mammal physiology, Dave worked on a wide range of research projects ranging from fish, bird and mammal population studies to experiments with biodiversity and prairie restoration. A lifelong fisherman and avid naturalist, he is now spending his retirement writing, fishing and traveling.